A GULL ON THE ROOF

Also by Derek Tangye and available in the NEL series

A DRAKE AT THE DOOR
A CAT IN THE WINDOW
LAMA
A DONKEY IN THE MEADOW
A CORNISH SUMMER

A Gull on the Roof

Derek Tangye

Sketches by
Jean Tangye

NEW ENGLISH LIBRARY
TIMES MIRROR

TO JEANNIE

First published in Great Britain by Michael Joseph Ltd. in March 1961
Five impressions before January 1963
Sixth impression January 1963

© Copyright 1961 by Derek Tangye

*

FIRST FOUR SQUARE EDITION July 1965
Reissued in this NEL edition February 1971
Reprinted December 1973

*

NEL Books are published by
New English Library Limited from Barnard's Inn, Holborn, London, E.C.1.
Made and printed in Great Britain by Hunt Barnard Printing Ltd.. Aylesbury, Bucks.

45000689 1

INTRODUCTION

I SAT down in our house overlooking the Thames at Mortlake and felt a soft, caressing rub at my ankle. Monty was saying in his feline fashion that he sympathised with me over the apprehension that was in my mind.

The humble earth must ever fly (wrote A. P. Herbert).
Round that great orange in the sky;
But, Monty, with devotion due
The home of Tangye turns round you.

An animal, as one grows older, plays the role of the teddy bear in childhood. He stirs those qualities which are best in one's character and is one's patient confessor in periods of distress. So it was with Monty. He was, for both Jeannie and myself, the repository of our secret thoughts.

My apprehension that evening was in reality an ally of the caution I had discarded, for in the morning we had set in motion our decision to leave London in favour of the bathless, paraffin-lit two-roomed cottage called Minack and six acres of uncultivated land on the coast between Penzance and Land's End. I had completed the settlement of my own affairs and Jeannie had handed in her resignation to the Chairman of the Savoy Hotel. Our livelihood now depended upon the creation of a flower farm from this desolate, beautiful country, aided not by any practical exerience, but only by our ignorance as to what lay ahead.

Jeannie's position at the Savoy was the epitome of a career girl's ambition, but it was because she was not career minded that she performed her duties so well. As Public Relations Officer of the Savoy, Claridges, Berkeley and Simpsons, she had a high salary, a large expense account and a multitude of friends. Her salient task had been to promote goodwill, and that was achieved not only by organising efficiently the daily routine of an office, but also by endearing herself to the great variety of people who pass through an international hotel.

'Absolute nonsense!' said the Chairman when she saw him, 'you're obviously tired and want a rest. Take six months holiday with pay' . . . then added: 'When you come back you will want to stay with us for ever.'

I could understand his scepticism for he had no knowledge of the months of reasoning which had brought us to this moment. He could only comprehend the fact she was throwing away a career of distinction in favour of a wild adventure which, after a short while, might appear as a misplaced enthusiasm.

He could not be expected to appreciate the sense of futility which perforce invades the kind of life we had been leading. The glamour and hospitality act as a narcotic, doping the finer instincts of living, and in the grey hours of early morning you lie awake painfully aware that you live in a flashy world where truth and integrity for the most part are despised, where slickness reigns supreme.

We found the pace too fast and any material rewards poor substitutes for the peace of mind which was sacrificed. The world of politics, journalism and entertainment in which we moved requires a ruthless zest for professional survival if you are to do so, and this neither of us now possessed. It is a world in which you cannot live on prestige alone for it is only the present that counts. We had come to distrust both the importance of the objectives and the methods used to achieve them; for it is a world in which acclaim, however transitory and gained at whatever moral cost, is valued in the same currency as the conquest of Everest.

The atmosphere corrodes the individual and it had been corroding Jeannie and me. The moment of self-criticism, the shame we felt for our arid minds, slipped into oblivion as soon as we were in the splash of another party, in a cuckoo land of mutual admiration and sudden rip-roaring friendships.

There was no decisive occasion when we decided to leave.

6

It was a host of occasions mingled into one, so that one day we suddenly realised our life was a spinning top, dizzily circling on one spot. We saw our fate, if we remained, in the men and women around us who had taken no heed of the barrier between youth and middle age, braying prejudiced views, dependent on values that toppled upside down, propping against a future which repeats endlessly the present, resembling worn playing cards. We could either drift on, or start again. We could either suffer the illusion our life was a contented one, remain within the environment we knew too well, or seek a freedom in a strange one.

We had been playing the game of looking for somewhere to settle whenever we had taken our holidays in Cornwall. We wanted a cottage with a wood near by and fields that went down to the sea, distant from any other habitation and remote from a countrified imitation of the life we were wishing to leave. Somewhere where we could earn a living and yet relish the isolation of a South Sea island, be able to think without being told what to think, to have the leisure to study the past, to live the present without interference.

It is a game which is perfectly harmless so long as no place you see fits your ideal. Once the two coincide the moment of decision arrives and it is no longer a game. This is what happened when Jeannie and I found Minack.

1

WE had set out, one May morning, from the inn in the Valley of Lamorna to walk westwards along the coast. We were on a week's holiday and as usual the carrot dangling before us on the walk was our imaginary home.

Lamorna was once the centre of quarrying and its beauty was incidental. The great blocks of granite were blasted from the cliff face beside the little harbour, transported in long wooden wagons pulled by teams of horses up and down the hills to Penzance where they were cut into the required shapes and shipped for building purposes all over Britain.

The name means valley by the sea, and it is now a sleepy wooded valley possessing the ethereal beauty, the lush vegetation and shimmering colours, the away from it all atmosphere which tempts people to believe that here is their earthly Nirvana. In the summer, of course, it erupts with a lava of holidaymakers yet, and this is the charm of Lamorna, there is no strident attempt to exploit these visitors. There is the inn, a small hotel, Ernie Walter's filling station and cafe, Daniel's place down in the Cove; and though a few cottages advertise bed and breakfast in their windows, one feels this is done out of courtesy rather than a desire to earn a living. Lamorna, then, is a pilgrimage of the day tripper and though the narrow road on a summer afternoon is choked with cars, charabancs and dust, the evening comes and the valley is silent again. In winter it is always silent except for the wind in the trees and the echo of the surf in the cove, and it becomes a valley to cure a cynic. The air is sweet with the scent of the violet plants which climb up the hillsides in neat cultivated rows, and as you walk along you will meet a picker, a basket of violets or anemones in either hand, taking them home to bunch. Or in the early spring when cities are still shivering, you will find the valley a factory of flowers with every inhabitant a picker or a buncher, sharing in the hectic race to harvest the daffodils before those 'up along' come into bloom. During the war growers had to surrender a large part of their daffodil ground to the growing of vegetables, and so they thew their bulbs at random in the woods. The effect in spring is as if the constellations had left their places in the sky for Lamorna woods, a myriad yellow lights peeping from the undergrowth, edging the sparkling stream beside moss-covered boulders, struggling through twining, unfriendly brambles.

The path we walked along was only a shadow of a path, more like the trodden run of badgers. Here, because there was no sign of habitation, because the land and the boulders and the rocks embraced the sea without interference, we could sense we were part of the beginning of time, the centuries of unceasing waves, the unseen pattern of the wild generations of foxes and badgers, the ageless gales that had lashed the desolate land, exultant and roaring, a giant harbour of sunken ships in their wake. And we came to a point, after a steep climb, where a great Carn stood balanced on a smaller one, upright like a huge man standing on a stool, as if it were a sentinel waiting to hail the ghosts of lost sailors. The track, on the other side, had tired of the undergrowth which blocked its way along the head of the cliff, for it sheered seawards tumbling in a zigzag course to the scarred grey rocks below. We stood on the pinnacle . . . the curve of Mount's Bay leading to the Lizard Point on the left, the Wolf Rock lighthouse a speck in the distance, a French crabber a mile off-shore, pale blue hull and small green sail aft, chugging through the white speckled sea towards Newlyn, and high above us a buzzard, its wings spread motionless, soaring effortlessly into the sky.

Jeannie suddenly pointed inland. 'Look!' she said, 'there it is!'

There was never any doubt in either of our minds. The small grey cottage a mile away, squat in the lonely landscape, surrounded by trees and edged into the side of a hill, became as if by magic the present and the future. It was as if a magician beside this ancient Carn had cast a spell upon us, so that we could touch the future as we could, at that moment, touch the Carn. There in the distance we could see our figures moving about our daily tasks, a thousand, thousand figures criss-crossing the untamed land, dissolving into each other, leaving a mist of excitement of our times to come.

We stood outside the cottage and stared; a Hans Andersen cottage with the primitive beauty of a crofter's home, sad and neglected as if it were one of the grey boulders in the wild land around. The walls seemed to grow out of the ground, great rocks fingering up the sides until they met the man placed stones, rough faced granite slabs bound together by clay. Once upon a time, it appeared to us, there might have been upstairs rooms and perhaps a roof of thatch; but now the roof was an uncouth corrugated iron jagged with holes, tilting so steeply that it resembled a man's cap pulled over his eyes; and prodding defiantly into the sky above it, as if ashamed of being associated with such ugliness, was a massive lichen-covered chimney. The poky windows peered from the darkness within, three facing the moorland and the sea, and two either side of the battered door which looked upon the unkempt once loved tiny garden. We pushed the door and it was unlocked. Wooden boards peppered with holes gnawed by rats covered the floor, and putting my hand through one of them I touched the wet earth. The walls were mustard yellow with old paper and though the area of the cottage was that of an old fashioned drawing-room it was divided into four rooms, matchbox thick divisions yielding the effect of privacy. At right angles to the door in a cavity of the wall beneath the chimney, an ancient Cornish range seared with rust, droppings of rats dirtying the oven, brandished the memories of forgotten meals. Above, the sagging thin boards of the ceiling drooped in curves, rimmed grey in patches from rain dripping through the roof. A cupboard faced the door and inside broken crockery lay on the shelves, a brown kettle without a lid, and a mug imprinted with a coloured picture of King George V and Queen Mary side by side. Musty with long absence of an inhabitant,

11

lugubrious with the crush of the toy sized rooms, the cottage seemed yet to shine with welcome; and we felt as if we had entered Aladdin's Cave.

Outside we stood by the corner of the cottage, the battered door facing climbing ground behind us, and looked down upon a shadow of a valley, gentle slopes, heading for the sea. Beyond was the Carn where we had stood, cascading below it a formation of rocks resembling an ancient castle, and in the distance across the blue carpet of sea the thin white line of breakers dashing against the shores of Prah Sands, Porthleven and Mullion. A lane drifted away from the cottage. On its right was a barn with feet thick walls in which were open slits instead of windows and on its left was a tumbled-down stone hedge, holding back the woods we had seen and the jungle-like growth, as policemen try to hold back a bursting throng. The lane led down to a stream, dammed into a pool by the density of the weeds which blocked its outflow, and then, a few yards on, petered out in a tangle of brushwood and gorse bushes. We could see that the cottage was only connected with civilisation by a track through a field.

There was another track which led towards the sea and, as it broke away from the environment of the cottage, we found roofless outbuildings, bramble covered stone walls, with blackthorn growing where once stood men and cattle sheltering from the weather. The track broke into a huge field or what we could see by the hedges was once a field but now had grown into part of the desolate moorland, then fell downwards to the top of the cliff. It was no ordinary cliff. It did not fall fearsomely sheer to the sea below but dropped, a jungle of thorns, gorse, elderberry trees and waist high couch grass, in a series of leaps to a rugged teaspoon of a bay; and as we stood there, somnolent gulls sitting on the rocks far below, we saw in our minds a giant knife slicing pocket meadows out of the rampaging vegetation, refashioning the cliff so that it resembled the neat pattern of daffodil and potato gardens that were grouped like hillside Italian vineyards at intervals along the coast. We saw in our minds not only a way of life, but also the means by which to earn a living. It was the sweet moment when the wings of enthusiasm take flight, when victory is untarnished by endeavour, the intoxicating instant when the urge for conquest obliterates the reality of obstacles, dissolving common sense, blanketing the possibilities of failure. We had found our imaginary home. If we were able to possess it the way stretched clear to our contentment.

Details about the cottage were told to us back at the inn. Mrs Emily Bailey who was then the innkeeper, and Tom her son who nursed the adjoining market garden but who now has taken her place – these two listened patiently to our excitement. It was the habit of holidaymakers to lean over the bar expounding their hopes of packing up jobs, seeking an answer as to where they could escape; and these words of good intentions were as familiar to Tom and Mrs Bailey as the good-byes at the end of holidays, a part of the holiday as splits and Cornish cream, a game of make-believe that was played for a fortnight, then forgotten for another year.

The cottage was on the land of a farm which belonged to one of the great Cornish estates. This Estate rented the farm to a large farmer who lived a few miles from Land's End who, in turn, sublet it out on a dairyman's lease. This lease was a relic of those days when Estates had difficulty in finding tenants for their farms. An established farmer would rent an unwanted farm, stock it with cattle and hire out each cow to a man of his own choosing who would occupy the farmhouse and farm the land. Hence this man, or dairyman as he was called, had no responsibility to the Estate for he was only a cowman. The responsibility of upkeep lay in the hands of the absentee farmer who, in this case, was a man called Harry Laity. As I lay awake that night he loomed like an ogre and, determined to call on him on the morrow, I experienced the same queasiness as I had felt before the interview for my first job.

We took the bus to a hamlet called Poljigga and found ourselves deposited at the end of a drive a mile long; a dusty, pot-ridden drive with the farmhouse eyeing us in the distance. We were absurdly nervous. Jeannie whose success was born from her ease with spangled names, and I whose duty it had been to have a weekly solitary interview with the Secretary of the Cabinet, walked along that drive, nervous as children visiting the headmaster. An over-sophisticated approach, a crude remark, sincerity sounding shallow because of lack of confidence, could batter our hopes for ever.

'What on earth do I say?' I said to Jeannie.

My passport, I thought, could be that I was a Cornishman. My ancestors had come from Brittany at the beginning of the fifteenth century, being descended from the Breton family of Tannegui du Chatel whose ruined castle still exists in the north-west corner of Finisterre. The Tangyes lived in obscurity in various parishes of West Cornwall until my grandfather, Richard, was born at Illogan near Redruth. His parents kept the village shop, and farmed a few acres near by where my great-grandfather followed the plough in Quaker dress and broad-brimmed hat. Richard and his brothers became engineers, and breasting the waves of the industrial revolution their inventiveness quickly brought them fame and fortune. Their success, they used to say, dated from the occasion when Isambard Brunel's huge vessel the *Great Eastern* obstinately refused to be launched from the dock at Millwall where it was built. Its length was nearly seven hundred feet, its breadth more than eighty, the height of the hull sixty, whilst its five funnels were a hundred feet high and six feet in diameter. It was intended to carry four thousand passengers, a crew of four hundred besides a mighty cargo – but there it was wedged high and dry on the stocks. It was then that the Tangye brothers produced their new invention the hydraulic jack, and to the excitement of the watching crowd, the vessel slid into the water. 'We launched the *Great Eastern*,' said Richard, 'and the *Great Eastern* launched us.'

My father was trained as a lawyer and he belonged to that group of men and women who, though without personal ambition, perpetually give their services to the community in unpaid but responsible jobs. He was, among other appointments, Joint Chairman of the Cornwall Quarter Sessions, a Deputy Lieutenant of the County, and organiser of the Cornwall Special Constabulary until he died in 1944.

He was easy among people and they could always endear themselves to him by enthusing over the loveliness of Glendorgal. Glendorgal, now a hotel kept by my brother Nigel, was our home on the north coast of Cornwall near Newquay and it has the most beautiful position imaginable; the house is low and rambling and stares up the wild north coast past Watergate Bay and Bedruthan Steps to Trevose Head in the far distance. Below the house, so close that you can throw a stone into it from the dining-room, is a sandy cove which is itself a dent in Porth Beach. Across this beach is Trevelgue Island, historic for its ancient burial grounds, though it is an island only by the length of the footbridge which connects it to the mainland. My father had a great love for this island but just before the war circumstances forced him to sell it. The buyers were the local Town Council and I remember the wrangling which went on during the negotiations. It centred round a public convenience. My father was aware of the Cornish habit of erecting ugly cement blockhouses in the most prominent situations without any regard to the visual effect on the beauty spot concerned. The island had always been open to the public but the Town Council, now that they were buying it, believed they could improve its amenities. They intended to erect a blockhouse on the island which would remain for ever a silhouetted sore against the view beyond. My father was adamant that this should not be done, and though in the end he won his point, it was only by sacrificing a large amount from the sum the Council had been prepared to pay.

My father delighted in affectionate surprises. When I was returning to London by train he would see me off at Newquay station, then race in his old Wolseley car the three miles to Quintrell Downs where he would stand at the railway crossing waving his pipe as the train rushed by. I remember another time, after my twenty-first birthday weekend, I and my friends had said good-bye to him at Glendorgal before returning to London by car and then found him, one hour and a half later, nonchalantly strolling on the Tamar Bridge at Launceston accompanied by Lance his old English sheepdog; by a round-about route he had raced to

15

the bridge to say good-bye again.

We walked apprehensively along the Laity drive, happily unaware that this was the first of our visits on the same errand. We were nervous, as actors are before a performance, but in our hearts we did not think we could fail. Our zest would smother the awkwardness of the introduction and, because we were accustomed to meeting strange people, we would soon be at our ease. We were wrong.

Harry Laity, whose robust enjoyment of life we were later to appreciate, eyed us as if we had escaped out of Broadmoor. We saw him first in the yard outside the farm-house watching the cows being brought in to milk; and I began to explain our mission while he stared at the cattle as they passed. I soon became aware that our presence was a nuisance and my confidence ebbed. This was not a situation which either of us had foreseen, and was not one that smooth manners could dissolve. We were out of our depth. The gambits on which we were accustomed to rely were as ineffective as a saddle on a wild pony; and as I stood there awkwardly beside him our plans, which to us seemed so important, became deformed, diminished by their reception into a scatterbrained foolishness.

The cattle disappeared to their milking, and he led us into the house and to the dining-room. Jeannie and I sat down with Harry Laity opposite, the bare dining-table like a frozen lake between us. I sat there and began to describe – defensively, falsely jovial – my Cornish background, our longing for a Cornish home, our plans for Minack. He stared at us, his eyes giving no clue to his thoughts, puffing a cigarette, replying to my leading questions with grunts and monosyllables. His attitude was unnerving. I began to overstress our case. The more unresponsive he was, the more talkative I became. I slithered into sounding like Uriah Heep. I felt myself acting like a gold prospector who, having found gold, was cunningly pretending he needed the land for another purpose. Handsome Harry as he was known in the neighbourhood was suspicious. He could not be expected to understand why I pleaded as if our lives depended upon his decision. It was beyond his comprehension why two people should wish to leave London for such a derelict, isolated, unwanted place as Minack.

We went away and waited, and visited him again. We wrote carefully worded letters. We enlisted the help of our mutual friends to put our case. We sat in our Mortlake home endlessly discussing the tactics which might penetrate the obstinacy of this man who held our future in his hands. We were at the door as soon as the postman knocked. Nothing. The weeks dragged into months. Silence.

And then, one November morning, we had a message to call on Harry Laity the next time we were in Cornwall. Jeannie was in bed with flu, but it was she who proposed we should take the night train to Penzance.

2

THE blessing of enthusiasm is its ability to deceive pleasantly. When Harry Laity told us we could live at Minack, it seemed that now the major obstacle had been overcome, our other problems would be solved without effort. And yet, the victory achieved, doubts soon began to enter my mind.

'We're intending to live in a wilderness,' I said to Jeannie, 'we have little in the bank and we haven't a clue as to how to grow anything. The world is littered with people who would *like* to do what we are wanting to do. Common sense stops them.'

We were, for instance, brushing aside the fact that we would have no legal security at Minack. The cottage, and a vaguely defined area of land, had been offered us at a low rent by the tenant of the farm but not by the Estate which owned it; hence we had no lease, yet in our zest to secure occupancy we had promised that all improvements would be at our expense. We convinced ourselves that once we had moved in, no one was likely to turn us out; and that conventional legal niceties, if pursued, might scare Harry Laity away from having anything to do with us. Long afterwards he told us we were right in our guesswork. He let us have Minack because he expected we would stay six months, then creep back to London, leaving a redecorated cottage behind.

The cottage, then, was now nominally ours though it was eighteen months before we were able to set off along the Great West Road to live there; but during this interval, as we continued our rackety life in London, there remained in our minds the picture of Minack, snug, untamed, remote, giving us the same sense of protection as a deep shelter in an air-raid. Whenever we had the time we dashed to its safety.

Our first visit was a week-end in November when we

introduced Monty to his new home. When I first met Monty I was allergic to cats, or rather, as we had never kept cats in our family and knew nothing about them, I pretended to be. He had been found, the last of a litter from a tortoiseshell, by Jeannie's mother in a hairdresser's at St Albans, and brought to Jeannie at the Savoy not long after we had been married. One day I walked unsuspectingly into her office and there on the floor, like a miniature foal trying to control his legs, was Monty. It was a few months after the battle of El Alamein.

I feigned my displeasure and as it was to be my task to take him back to our house overlooking the finishing post at Mortlake, I insisted I would drop him over Hammersmith Bridge. But we passed the bridge and he was still in the basket, and though I swore he would only be a kitten cat, he slept that night on our bed. From that day he shared with us doodle-bugs, rockets, a bomb on the house, wore a light blue ribbon each Boat-race day, sat for hours at night on the window-sill waiting for our returns, made many hours happy with his purrs, and was always universally admired.

To call him a ginger cat would be a mundane description. The postman at Minack, when he first saw him, called him red – after the red cats of Zennor. There is a legend that a woman many years ago came to the village of Zennor, on the north coast of the Land's End peninsula, and announced she was going to breed tigers. The local authorities, not unnaturally, stepped in and forbade her to do so. The woman thereupon declared that if she could not breed tigers she would breed a red cat as fierce as a tiger, and now if you go from St Ives to Zennor it is the strangest fact that nearly every cat has a tinge of red. But Monty was not red. He had a snow white shirt front, magnificent whiskers, white paws except for a front one which had a puddle of orange on it, while the rest of his person was covered with a semi-Persian fur the colour of bracken in autumn. 'Like a fox,' a farmer said, 'and you'll have to be careful when the hounds are around.'

We had left London after lunch on a Friday and in the back of the car were a mattress and blankets, a Valor stove, other camping equipment, and Monty in a wicker basket specially bought for the occasion. The basket was my idea. I had visions of Monty escaping from the car and disappearing into the countryside; but by the time we reached Andover he was clearly losing his temper, miaowing his head off and clawing at the sides of the basket in fury. 'Perhaps he wants a walk,' I said. We found a quiet spot off the main road, carefully lifted the lid, and fitted him with a blue harness and lead which had also been bought for the occasion. His fury swept the quiet spot like a storm and he would not budge as I pulled at the lead. 'Let him be,' said Jeannie, 'let's get back in the car and let him sit on my lap.' In a few minutes he was purring contentedly and staring with interest out of the window at the passing scene; and the wicker basket and the lead and the harness have now been for years in the attic as a discarded monument to my foolishness in treating him as a cat who did not know how to travel. He came several times by car before staying at Minack for ever, and once by first-class sleeper. I was at Minack on my own and was expecting Jeannie down for the week-end. I was on the platform at Penzance when the night train drew in, and I saw her waving excitedly from a window. I went up to the door of her carriage and she said: 'Come and look what I've got in my sleeper!' I opened the sliding door, and there on the bunk was Monty. She had been dining at the Savoy when she suddenly had the whim of bringing Monty with her. She rushed back to Mortlake, found him by torchlight walking along the garden wall, wrapped him in a rug and carried him to a taxi. At Paddington he behaved like any prudent conspirator as he was smuggled into the train, and Jeannie awoke every now and then during the night to find him purring peacefully beside her. He stayed on with me for a few days after Jeannie returned; then we drove back together to Mortlake.

It was nearly midnight, on that first visit, when the three of us reached Penzance. A gale was blowing in from the sea and as we drove along the front cascades of spray drenched the car as if coming from a giant hose. We crossed Newlyn Bridge, then up steep Paul Hill and along the winding road

21

past the turn to Lamorna Valley; then up another hill, Boleigh Hill, where King Athelstan fought the Cornish ten centuries ago. Rain was whipping the windscreen when we turned off the road along a lane, through the dark shadows of a farm, until it petered out close to the cliff's edge. I got out and opened a gate, then drove bumpily across a field with the headlights swathing a way through a carpet of escaping rabbits. This, the back entrance to Minack, was the way we had to use until the bramble covered lane was opened up again; and after I pulled up beside a stone hedge, we still had two fields to scramble across in the darkness and the rain and the gale before we reached the cottage.

I lit a candle and the light quivered on the peeling, yellow papered walls. Everything was the same as the day we first pushed open the door; the ancient Cornish range, the pint sized rooms with their matchbox thick divisions, the wooden floor peppered with holes – only it was raining now and above the howl of the gale was the steady drip, drip of water from the leaking roof.

We didn't care. The adventure had begun.

The phase in which daydreams had to be turned into facts had also begun. The romantic, escape-from-it-all atmosphere in which we had battled for the possession of Minack was now dissolving into the uncanny realism of victory. I had the same sense of living in the third dimension as the day when I enlisted in the Army and exchanged emotional patriotism for the discipline of the unknown. We could no longer talk of what we were going to do, we had to act; and the actions increasingly enmeshed us in a condition of living from which there was no turning back. As our first visit was succeeded by others, individuals entered our lives who pushed us forward linking our future with their present, as if they were pylons of a bridge. First we had looked for a bolt-hole from the kind of life we were leading, then we relished the emotion of its discovery, now we met the responsibilities of success. We found ourselves faced with a challenge that defeated our brittle egos, that was only to be accepted by the selves within us who found tranquillity in integrity.

Ashley Thomas was the carpenter in our village of St

Buryan. Tubby, twinkling eyes, always wearing a peaked cloth cap to cover his bald head, he reminded Jeannie of Happy in Snow White and the Seven Dwarfs. His family had been carpenters in St Buryan for over two hundred years and craftsmanship was his second nature. And along with his tradition of skill was a quixotic nature akin to the carpenter of a neighbouring village who, after years of never sending out a bill, piled them all in his yard a few weeks before he died – and set them alight. Ashley Thomas never sent out an account within three years of the work being completed; then he would present it most courteously in person while the account itself was a masterpiece of script, a scroll it should be called, in which every nut, nail and inch of wood was meticulously tabulated.

Ashley Thomas looked around the debris of the cottage, notebook in hand with a pencil behind his ear, and promptly provided the assurance that order could soon be created. Our plans were not ambitious. A new roof, that was essential; the thin boards of the ceiling could remain but the matchbox thick divisions had to be ripped away, providing us with one large room in which to live and a small one that would be our bedroom. The Cornish range was useless so a modern stove that both cooked and gave warmth would be its substitute. The rat-gnawed planks covering the floor would be torn up and in their place a damp-resisting cement flooring would layer the earth. The mustard yellow paper would be peeled off the walls, and the crater-pitted slabs lime-washed white. The battered front door would be removed, replaced by one divided in half, like that of a stable. There would be no sink or bath and the lavatory would remain an Elsan, posted in a hut like a sentry box thirty yards from the cottage. Water, until we could sink a well, was going to be a tricky affair. We would have to collect the rain from the roof into a water-butt or fill a jug from the stream; but in the summer the stream dried up, and if the water-butt was empty as well, we would have to go three miles to the village tap in St Buryan square. 'Never mind,' said Ashley Thomas, looking at Jeannie, 'it's lovely at Minack in summer and lack of water won't worry you . . .

23

but how you'll stand it in winter I just don't know.'

While Ashley Thomas provided the guiding hand within, Tom Bailey from the inn at Lamorna acted as adviser without. He arrived at the cottage on a drenching afternoon when the sky seemed to have changed places with the sea. Clad in oilskins and sou'wester he looked as if he had come from a lifeboat. 'Come on,' he said, 'let's walk round' — and he said it as if the sun was shining. Tall and square, Tom was the man the villagers called on first in times of trouble. He had the dark cadaverous Cornish good looks with a watch in his eyes like that of a sailor, as if much of his life had been spent staring at the signs of the weather in the skies. He had been head gardener of a neighbouring estate before he began his own market garden, and his lifetime experience of growing was at the disposal of anyone who sought it. He was gentle in his manner and never dogmatic, and the advice he gave came hesitantly as if he considered it an insult to correct, however ignorant might be his listener. And he had the gift, despite his knowledge of technical difficulties, of fanning enthusiasm instead of blighting it with past evidence of personal failure.

'That'll make a nice meadow,' he said, looking at the bog which sided the wood below the cottage. It was the second of our brief visits and, despite the rain, we had spent the morning in this bog channelling an escape route for the water using a broken cup and a trowel. I do not know what we expected to achieve except to re-experience the pleasure of bucket and spade on a sea-shore. The task ahead was enormous and though Tom was right, and it did in the end make a nice meadow, it took two years of experimenting and two hundred yards of underground drain pipes before it was dry enough to grow a crop. Then we grew violets and sent away to market five hundred bunches in six months.

'That's yours?' He was looking at the ancient building bordering the lane, half of which was a stable, half a general purpose shed. It was not ours, only the roofless, age-stricken buildings came within our agreement. 'It's John's,' I replied.

John also was a new arrival — as Harry Laity's dairyman he had come to live at the farm at the top of the hill and was

24

our nearest neighbour. The land he worked dovetailed into ours. We, of course, had accepted the uncultivated land. His consisted of the weirdly shaped, beautiful meadows that bordered the cliff and ran down to the sea's edge, and the green fields which lipped the pocket garden of the cottage. He had called one morning when we were cooking breakfast on the oil stove.

'You're John,' I said, and shook his hand in welcome. He was squat and powerfully built like a miner. He had a round face with skin coarsened by the open air. His eyes were grey and they looked at me as if he was saying to himself: 'I wonder how long these people are going to stick it here.' He wore an old raincoat and a mottled brown cloth cap aslant on the back of his head, showing his black hair tinged with grey; a cigarette hung out of the corner of his mouth and he fiddled a foot with an imaginary stone. And as I talked with him I suddenly became aware of a warning emotion within me for which my town conception of a country life had not prepared me. There was a hint of challenge in his manner. It was as if I had had a punch on the nose to remind me we were amateurs who had a hazy, paradise notion of country life that had no relation to reality. We did not belong. We were as out of place in the kind of life we were intending to lead as John would have been in the Savoy Grill. I could see him wondering what mystery had brought us here. Why, because we possessed smooth ways, did we think we could exist in a land where skill was the product of generations of struggle? We were typical city dwellers who had the conceit to believe it would be easy. He had seen them come and go before, and we would be no exception. There would be the customary froth of enthusiasm as we put the cottage in order, the showing off to up-a-long friends, the token effort of manual work, the gradual boredom with discomfort. Anyhow *she* won't last. Then, and I could sense the question revolving in his mind: 'Who will get the cottage?' His visit had a salutary effect on us for it promised the stimulus of battle, the realisation that we were going to be watched and judged and expected to fail. He was another pylon of the bridge.

We led Tom Bailey to the little wood, a forest of blackthorn and elm tree saplings with grey boulders heaving up in groups between them. 'Cut them down and dig up their roots,' he said, 'and by dodging them boulders you'll have three, maybe four meadows out of here. They'll be sheltered . . . be all right for daffodils.' And all this time we were pestering him with elementary questions. What varieties of daffodils would be best for us? How do you grow them? What about violets . . . and anemones . . . and potatoes? We left the wood and took the path to the big field and the cliff, into the scrub, the waste-land smothered with gorse and brambles where one day, we hoped, the crops would grow which Tom described to us. 'Mind,' he said, 'everyone will tell you different and no season is ever the same . . . but this is how I find it.'

There are several thousand different varieties of daffodils and narcissi but only a comparative few are recognised in the markets as established commercial successes – such as the yellow trumpet King Alfred, Magnificence, Carlton, Rembrandt, and a hundred or so others. Some of these are early varieties, some middle season, some late, and the aim of the grower is to have a succession of blooms from the end of January to the end of March, usually ending up with the white narcissi such as Cheerfulness, a double white bloom with an exquisite scent. The normal custom is to buy bulbs by weight which means the bulbs will be of different sizes – most will flower the first year but others will take a year or so to reach flowering size. If you buy by numbers you can expect all the bulbs to flower the first year but, quite apart from it being a much more expensive way of doing things, you run the risk of the bulbs taking a rest the following year with the result you pick few flowers. In any case bulbs are expensive. Cornish growers usually buy their bulbs from Holland or the Isles of Scilly and the price, of course, varies according to the variety; normally, standard types such as King Alfred, cost about £150 a ton. The big growers plant bulbs with a plough, placing them two or three inches apart within the rows: the small growers, in their cliff meadows, use a shovel and, when the time comes to dig them out, a special clawed digger. Seven tons average the acre and a good yield per ton is 28,000 flowers.

When you have bought and planted your stock the hazards begin. A gale may blow up during the week the blooms are ready to be harvested, and although they are always picked in bud the damage incurred as the buds rub against each other in the wind may result in all your efforts ending up in the compost heap. Then there is eel-worm and the bulb fly, two pests which are as common as household flies and one of which is usually the answer to home gardeners who wonder why their bulbs have disappeared. Eel-worm, microscopic in size, wriggles through the soil attacking a plantation like an invincible army, burrowing into the bulbs and destroying them; and after such an attack, since eel-worm hangs around feeding on certain kinds of weeds, you have to leave the ground empty of bulbs for seven years. 'In fact,' said Tom, 'once you have eel-worm in the soil you seldom get completely rid of it. You can only check it.' Yet if you have the luck not to have eel-worm there is nothing to stop the bulbs being attacked by the bulb-fly for it is on the wing every year. There is a small bulb-fly and a large one but they both look like any other flying insect of the spring. The fly lays its eggs in the neck of the bulb and the larvae proceeds to mature within the bulb, feeding on its tissues until it is destroyed into a sticky mess. Hence bulbs should be dug up every three years and given hot water sterilisation treatment before being split from each other and replanted in September; an hour of this treatment will kill the larvae of the fly, three hours the eel-worm. If the bulbs are cared for in this way they will increase considerably in numbers; if they are left as they are generally left in a garden; they will gradually die away and the capital you have invested will be lost. 'The trouble is,' said Tom, 'there always seems something more urgent to do than digging up bulbs and planting them again.'

The flowers are picked when the buds have dropped at right angles to the stem, and they are brought into the packing shed and put into pails of water. If the weather is cold, there has to be a gentle heat in the shed to help burst the buds open. Then, when their petals are spread they are bunched and sent away to the markets. Every grower has a salesman in each of several markets and he is charged ten per cent on the sales plus a market charge for the handling of each box. Some growers have their own boxes, others hire boxes from the salesmen. In any case the grower pays the railway freight charges to whichever market he sends. In fact a grower has to pay twenty per cent in commission, boxes, market charges and freight, out of any price he receives for his flowers.

Tom said that violets provided his bread and butter. They are a cheap crop to grow because each year stock consists of the runners pulled off the previous season's plants. They are planted in May and June, fifteen inches apart and about the same distance between the rows. The plants have bushed out by September and have begun flowering by the end of the month, continuing to do so through the winter months to April. There is an average weekly picking of twelve dozen bunches for every thousand plants – twenty violets and two leaves making up a bunch. Up to fifteen thousand plants go to an acre but, Tom warned, such was the time and labour involved in picking and bunching, no small grower could manage such a number. He himself usually had four thousand plants, growing a variety called Governor Herrick which, though it has very little scent, is prolific in flowering and last very well once picked. He had no use for the pale-coloured, sweet-scented Princess of Wales because it was difficult to grow, bloomed scantily, and fetched no higher price in the market.

Anemones are more difficult to grow and more expensive, but they are as much part o. a Cornish market garden as bacon in a gocer's. The type most in demand in the markets is the De Caen variety, single blooms of multi-colours, and although some growers sow seed, the majority plant corms early in July. Seed is cheaper to buy but this economy is cancelled out by the extra labour involved. Good corms cost around fifteen shillings a thousand and eighty thousand go to an acre – the whole crop being ploughed into the ground at the end of the season. Their flowering period is the same as violets but they are liable to downy mildew which can devastate them, especially in a period of muggy weather when soft misty rain covers the Land's End peninsula – and as the spores of this mildew stay in the soil, anemones must not be grown in the same ground more than once in four years. 'Last year,' said Tom, 'I lost the lot because it was so wet before Christmas.' Frost, of course, sometimes damages them but as Tom explained, a frost hard enough to wipe out the plants seldom strikes West Cornwall. Anemones like a lot of lime in the ground and corms must be planted after the ground has been firmed, only a couple of inches deep and the same distance apart; and you must allow at least twenty inches between rows to enable the pickers to walk up and down without bruising the foliage. Mice sometimes do a great amount of damage. They nip off the buds as they break ground, then carry them off to the hedge where they tear off the petals and eat the heart of the flower. You can find little piles of these petals around every anemone field. The flowers are picked when the bud is just beginning to break. You must on no account send flowers to market which are 'blown' or full open, and this is very difficult to prevent in warm weather. If all goes well you should be able to send throughout the season an average of four dozen bunches a week for every five thousand corms you have planted.

Tom tempered these details with caution. He told us not to accept them as the gospel of the expert because the problems of market gardening were as numerous as a football permutation. Every season provides a different set of circumstances, and there is always an element which no one has ever experienced before. You are at the mercy of gluts and the weather, and they can knock you for six just when you think the season is going to be a good one.

We were now standing in the middle of our big field. It used to be called the cemetery field because at the bottom of it, the old cows and horses of neighbouring farms used to be buried. We were standing at the ridge half-way down – the top half sloped fairly gently, the bottom half suddenly dipped below the ridge until it levelled out just before the cliff. 'That top piece,' said Tom, looking at the upper half, 'that wouldn't take long to break if you had someone to help. Then you can hire a man with a plough and work up the land, then get a few potatoes in by March. Couldn't expect much but it would clean the ground and be a start.'

The growing of new potatoes held a fascination for us. There was past enjoyment of their flavour and the prospect of producing a crop so far ahead of the rest of the country that it had the merits of a delicacy; besides, stories had been told to us of small fortunes being made out of the pocket cliff meadows between Penzance and Land's End – 'the earliest potato land in England' it was called. Potatoes appeared easy to grow. In fact they seemed to be the answer to the amateur's prayers – hard manual work but no specialised skill, the warm climate and high prices ensuring a handsome profit. They would be the first corner stone of our income, so we then thought, as soon as we had the cultivated land in which to grow them. Hence Tom's suggestion suited us well.

Seed potatoes are delivered in the early winter and the varieties have names like Sharpe's Express, Home Guard, Arran Pilot, May Queen. When the seed arrives the potatoes are picked out and carefully placed eye-end up side by side in special wooden trays. They stay like this indoors until planting time, and by then they will have grown shoots a couple of inches long. The larger potatoes are then cut between the shoots so that there are two or even three sections which can grow on into plants. The planting is done in February and early March and, given good weather, the crop will be ready to draw at the beginning of May; and for every ton planted three or four tons should be harvested. The work, because the meadows are steep and small, has to be done by hand labour. Turning the ground in the autumn, planting the seed, digging out the crop – is all achieved by the use of the long-handled Cornish shovel. The seed potatoes are carried down the cliff, the harvest up. Thus every stage is identical to that in use a century ago; but we gladly accepted the prospect of what, in due course, would be our wearisome task, because of the anticipated financial returns.

We were assured that whereas a ton of seed potatoes cost £20, the cliff early new potatoes sold at an average of £70 a ton. It seemed to us we had found an El Dorado.

We looked expectantly at the land in which Tom proposed we should grow our first crop. It was late in the year to order the seed so there would not be time to 'shoot' them in the trays, and they would have to be planted 'blind'; but the first step was to find someone to take charge, to prepare the land, plant the potatoes and then look after them. That evening we went up to St Buryan village to seek the advice of Jim Grenfell, a Pickwickian figure who presides at the inn with the slow measured courtesy of the days of coach and horse rather than of motor cars. Jim soon found Harry, a rabbit catcher; and Harry, over seventy, wiry with bright blue eyes and a drooping white moustache, promised that if we left our problems in his hands, all would be well.

That spring as we toiled in London, we thought of our growing potatoes as one might think of a racehorse in training for a great race – and on each visit to Minack we dashed on arrival to stare at their progress. They developed so green and flourishing, five hundred weight had been planted and Home Guard was the variety, that we began contentedly estimating what our profit might be; and when Harry proclaimed the crop would be ready to draw the following week, I promised to come down and help. I left London at three in the morning and reached Penzance at ten – and on arrival I called at the wholesaler who had promised to market the crop.

'I've just driven down from London,' I said, with the rush of the journey still filling my ears, 'and I'm going on now to start digging the crop. You can expect me back this afternoon with a load.'

'Driven down specially from London?'

The man glared at me, and threw the stub of his cigarette viciously on to the pavement outside his shop.

'You must be mad . . . there's a glut of potatoes. They're not worth a penny a pound.'

*   *

In August Tommy Williams entered our lives and became the last pylon of the bridge. I met him first striding down Market Jew Street in Penzance one Saturday afternoon, wearing a Harris Tweed suit, a smart trilby, and smoking a cigar. He looked more like a wealthy farmer than a labourer who had spent his life around a cowshed, and I understood why I had been told I could not fail to recognise him if I saw him. He was very tall with a fine, thin looking face and brown eyes which gazed gently at you except when, and this I later found to be the case, he became roused; and then they would resemble those of an excited evangelist. He lived alone in a caravan near St Buryan and on the walls hung pictures which he had bought in local curiosity shops. 'I have a Constable,' he said proudly that first day I met him, 'a genuine Constable . . . and a Stradivarius!' His eyes gleamed. 'It's broken but it can be mended!'

Shortly before my encounter with him – after a particularly rowdy argument with his employer – he made it known throughout the district that he would do no more regular work, only casual work and on days which suited him. This attitude admirably coincided with mine as I was looking for a man who would work two or three days a week at Minack throughout the winter so that, when in early spring we came down permanently to live, the foundations of our future endeavours would have been laid.

He was undaunted by what he found he had to do. With eyes of knowledge instead of wishful thinking he mapped the whereabouts of meadows in the undergrowth. He was impatient to slash the saplings and the brambles which blocked the lane. He talked of rebuilding the old roofless buildings and rerouting the course of the stream. He rushed out his plans as if he was drawing zest from the prospect of showing others what he was capable of achieving when left on his own. And then, during the winter, he sent us progress reports:

'I am pleased to inform you that I have trimmed down all the hedges round top and bottom. I have burned the trimmings and been around the field hedges and put back all small stones. I have cut the trees back around the two home meadows and stacked branches around hedges to keep out cattle. The little potato house meadow will be a nice meadow when I've finished breaking it. I have the thorns around the hedges for fences and windbreaks. There is quite sunny weather at Minack between showers. Well, that is all for the present. Tommy Williams.'

Then came the final report at the end of March, a few days before we were due to arrive:

'I have moved the stones in the front garden so that there are four beds instead of two. I have borrowed wallflowers from my cousin. They are in flower and taken well. Also primrose plants from the cliff. Makes the garden cheerful and I hope you will be pleased.'

And we *were* pleased.

3

JEANNIE'S friends looked out of their own personal windows and judged her decision according to the view they were accustomed to see.

'My dear, what are you going to *do* all day?'

'If *only* I had the same courage!'

'Are you *sure* you're not going to miss all the fun?'

'I'll take a bet you're back in six months!'

Those in the tight little world of parties, American Bars and gossipy sensations, disliked the idea of one of their number deserting – the justice of their lives was being questioned, an end had come into sight when they felt only safe in prolonged beginnings. Hence they interpreted her decision by complicated explanations, and gained satisfaction in their certainty she would soon be back.

Those who had never tasted the flavour of mixing with celebrities found her decision incomprehensible. She led the life of a modern fairy princess yet she was giving it up. She must be out of her mind, and they looked at her as if she were an oddity in a zoo.

There were others who envied her. These, captured by their own success, could only reason that she was showing the courage they believed they lacked themselves. Courage, in their view, was required if you are going to break the routine of butterfly pleasures – whereas Jeannie only saw in her choice a way of escape. We were both, in fact, taking the easy way out towards reaching our personal horizon of living time slowly.

We first met one evening at the Savoy in an air-raid. I had written a travel book called *Time was Mine* and my first words to her were abrupt: 'You're just the person I have been wanting to meet. Can you manage to get my book on the bookstall?'

I had written in this book of a man called Jeffries, a weird mountain of a man, whom I had met on a Japanese boat sailing from Sydney to the Far East, and who, as it proved, was a link between me and Jeannie. I used to sit on deck till late at night listening to the stories of nefarious life, leaning over the ship's rail, the soft breeze in our faces, watching the passing shadows of the islands along the Barrier Reef. It was the spring of 1939 and he was on his way to a job in the shipyards of Hong Kong.

'I once studied with Cheiro the astrologer and palmist, he said on one occasion. 'He told me I would never be any good, but then I was never able to tell him his judgement was wrong . . . you see, I worked out on my own that he would die when he was sixty-eight. And he died on his sixty-eighth birthday.'

As it turned out many of the prophecies Jeffries made to me during the voyage were proved false by events. There would be no war. Chamberlain would be Prime Minister for a further five years and so on. But one evening he asked whether I would be prepared to have my own hand read. I was not very keen because I had always remembered the distress of my mother who, when she was thirty, was told by a palmist that my father would die when she was forty-one. She said it was the most agonising year of her life for she never could get the prophecy out of her mind. However, I agreed and we sat down in a corner of the deck lounge, glasses of saki on the table beside us, and I watched Jeffries study my palm in his ape-like hands. Later I wrote in my diary what he said – among other things that I would marry in 1943, that my wife would be smaller than myself and dark, and that her initials would be J.E. . . .

Jeannie arranged for my book to be on the bookstall and in celebration I asked her out to dinner. The River Room, with its windows bricked up against bomb blast, was the Savoy restaurant in those days and we sat in a corner while the band of Carroll Gibbons played to a crowded dance floor in the background.

I happened to ask her whether she had any other Christian names beside Jean. And she said: 'The awful name of Everald.' I looked at her across the table. 'Do you mind saying that again?' She appeared puzzled, 'My full name is Jean Everald Nicol.' Two years later in 1943, we were married.

The American *Look* Magazine called Jeannie 'the prettiest publicity girl in the world'; and when it was announced she was leaving the Savoy, the newspapers wrote about her as if they were saying good-bye to a star. A columnist in the *Daily Mail* described her as slim, colleen-like, with green eyes and dark hair

' . . . who seems so young, innocent and delicately pretty that you couldn't imagine her saying "Boo" to the smallest and silliest goose. But Jean has said "Boo" to all sorts of important people including tough American correspondents.

'For ten years she has been a key woman at that international rendezvous of film stars, politicians, maharajahs, financiers, business men and what have you – the Savoy Hotel.

'She is about to quit the post of publicity boss or public relations officer for the Savoy, Berkeley and Claridge's. Her job consisted not only of keeping those hotels before the public but in stopping indiscreet stories from appearing in the newspapers and sometimes in protecting timid guests from the glare of publicity. Now that is a job requiring tact, intelligence and charm, and Jean has all three qualities.

'Who stopped the story about the colonel (with D.S.O.) who was working in the kitchens of the Savoy from getting into the papers? Jean Nicol. Who arranged Dior's first interview in this country? The same girl. When Ernie Pyle the famous American war correspondent (they made a film about him) was going off to his death in the Pacific he had his last lunch in London with Jean. He told her sadly: 'I'll never see you again. There's been too much luck in my life, and it's exhausted.'

'Close friend of Danny Kaye, Tyrone Power, Gertrude Lawrence, Bob Hope, Bing Crosby . . . there isn't a famous name in the past decade that doesn't know Jean.

'Well, she is going to retire for she thinks that ten years is enough to spend in the glare of London's West End. And she is right.'

We left Mortlake on a sunny April morning when the tide was pushing its way up the river, creeping into the inlets of the riverside like an octopus feeling with its tentacles. On the steps of the Ship, beer mugs in hand, a group stood ready to wave us good-bye. On their right loomed the Brewery, and on their left an empty space, an elm tree, and the house with the roof like a dunce's cap which we were leaving. The act of departure spares only the light hearted, and as I carried out our belongings, sticking them in the Land Rover, I found myself thinking of that ardour seven years before with which we came to this house; for it was with this ardour, dressed up in the new clothes, that we were going away. I looked up at the windows and thought of our happiness which would always live within the rooms; the unfinished sentences of gay conversations, raised glasses, sweet moments when endeavour had met its reward, affection like suffused sunlight warming the company of friends. I saw poised in my mind the fragments of other people's lives, lost perhaps by them, for ever attached to me . . .

Bob Capa, the wayward brilliant photographer, who was killed in Indo China was there, leaning against the door, his sombre face brightened by a stick of bombs falling across Duke's Meadows, cigarette drooping from his lips, quietly, with broken accent calling: 'Coming nearer, coming nearer' . . . a startled A. P. Herbert on a November night, whisky glass in hand, hearing the S.O.S. on the *Water Gypsy*'s hooter; the tide had gone out and the crew had awoken when she tilted on her side . . . George Slocombe on a winter's afternoon standing with his back to the fire, red-bearded like an apostle, praising the virtues of France . . . Baron hitching a camera under his withered arm before photographing Monty; 'Come on Monty, give us a smile' . . . Gertrude Lawrence, a cockney again, boisterously shouting the Cambridge crew to victory . . . Carroll Gibbons drawling the song *People will say we're in love* as he played at our small piano . . . Alec Waugh standing on the steps looking at the empty river: 'Your last Boat Race party . . . it was the best.' We had come to this house believing it would be our home for always, yet here we were setting off again, packing away past hopes and ambitions, disappointments and victories, buoyantly confident that we now knew better. 'A chapter of my life was closed', wrote Somerset Maugham when he left Tahiti, 'and I felt a little nearer to inevitable death.'

We were aware, too, that departure meant a crack in the lives of those who cared for us. Jeannie would no longer be calling in to see her parents nor would I be able to have the almost daily, hour long conversations with my mother. I was never unsettled by age difference with either of my parents. My father kept a perpetual eye on his own youth, and so never grew old in his approach to me and my two brothers. My mother's philosophy had been to hold up a mirror to the happiness of the three of us, and gain her own in the reflection. When I was a schoolboy I said proudly to a small friend: '*My* mother would walk five miles with a heavy suitcase if it would help me or my brothers.' The childish boast always remained true.

The canvas hood of the Land Rover bulged like a kitbag ; . . . an armchair, suitcases, books, pots and pans, blankets, a camp bed, an ironing board. They piled high behind us as we sat ready to start . . . my mother whom we were taking to my aunt's house on the way, Jeannie with Monty on her lap, and myself at the wheel. And as I let out the clutch and slowly moved away, we could only laugh with those who were waving us good-bye.

'I hope you'll get there!' was the last I heard as I turned the corner.

I was on the road to the West again, a road which from my childhood had been part of my life. I used to drive to Glendorgal, our family home, as casually as I drove from Victoria to Kensington. My father saying: 'When in 1903 I drove a car to Cornwall for the first time, a donkey and cart actually passed me on this hill.' My mother: 'Three weeks after my first driving lesson I set off for Glendorgal. We had a puncture at Honiton but there was no garage anywhere near and we had to send to Exeter to find someone to repair it.' And myself: 'Here at Amesbury we had a smash with a Baby Austin . . . on my twenty-first birthday weekend we drove through the night and had breakfast at that café . . . I bought an evening paper at this corner shop and learnt the *Royal Oak* had been sunk . . . the car broke down

39

here and I spent the night in that gateway . . . I was gonged on this stretch . . . ' Scores of incidents so vivid in my mind that it seemed to me, as I travelled this road again, that I had 'time regained'.

The full moon was waiting to greet us at Minack, a soft breeze came from the sea and the Lizard light winked every few seconds across Mount's Bay. An owl hooted in the wood and afar off I heard the wheezing bark, like a hyena, of a vixen. A fishing boat chugged by, a mile off shore, its starboard light bright on the mast. It was very still. The boulders, so massive in the day, had become gossamer in the moonlight, and the cottage, so squat and solid, seemed to be floating in the centuries of its past.

I said to Jeannie: 'Let's see if Monty will come for a walk.'

He came very slowly down the lane, peering suddenly at dangers in the shadows, sitting down and watching us, then softly stepping forward. His white shirt-front gleamed like a lamp. He sniffed the air, his little nose puzzling the source of the scents of water weeds, bluebells and the sea. He found a log and clawed it, arching his back. He heard the rustle of a mouse and he became tense, alert to pounce. I felt as I watched him that he was an adventurer prying his private unknown, relishing the prospect of surprise and of the dangers which would be of his own making. We paused by the little stream, waiting for him to join us, and when he did, he rubbed his head affectionately against my leg, until suddenly he saw the pebbles of moonlight on the water. He put out a paw as if to touch them.

'I'll pick him up and carry him over.'

But when I bent down to do so he struggled free of my grasp – and with the spring of a panther he leapt across, and dashed into the shadows beyond.

'Well done!' we cried, 'well done!'

This little stream where it crosses the lane as if it were the moat of Minack, halting the arrival of strangers, greeting us on our returns, acting as the watch of our adventures, was given a name that night.

Monty's Leap.

We awoke the following morning to the sun streaming through the curtainless windows, to the distant murmur of the sea, to a robin's song hailing another day, and the delicious sensation that there was no frontier to our future. If our watches stopped what did it matter? An hour, a day, a week could pass . . . there was no barrier to which we were advancing, no date on a calendar which glared at us from a distance. No telephone to shiver us into expectation. No early morning noises, a far off factory hooter, the first rumble of traffic, the relentless roar of a Tube . . . no man made alarms to jerk us into the beginning of another day. No newspaper shoved under the door. No clatter of milk bottles. Time to think, time to read. Go down to the rocks and stare vacantly at the sea. Perform insignificant, slowly achieved tasks – weeding the garden, mending a bolt on the door, sticking photographs in an album – without conscience nagging us with guilt. Take idle walks, observe the flight of a raven, the shifting currents of the sea, the delicate shades of moss. Travel the hours on horseback. Timelessness, isolation and simplicity creating the space which would protect us from the past. The hazy happiness of the present guiding our future.

I got up, collected a jug and went down to the stream. I had invited Monty to come with me but he would not budge. I picked him up and put him down in the garden, but within a second he had rushed indoors again. He behaved in this manner for several days, hating the daylight and only venturing out in the dark, and then if we accompanied him. It was difficult to understand his behaviour for on his previous brief visits, though he had never wandered far, he had always kept his nerve. A week later, however, he gained his self-confidence after meeting a baby rabbit face to face outside the front door. He seized it by the neck, brought it into the cottage while I was having breakfast, and deposited it at my feet – alive. Henceforth every tuft of grass was a potential rabbit and every capture brought to us for our admiration; and instead of having to lure him outside, we used to spend much of our time searching for his whereabouts.

While I fetched the water Jeannie went up to the patch of ground where we had fixed up a wired run for the chickens. We had always kept chickens at Mortlake where they lived in a disused air-raid shelter and in a run that was messy with mud. Now they had a house of their own and, although the site was open to the four winds of heaven, they had grass to scratch, legions of succulent insects to peck, and farm chicken food to eat instead of the sticky mash which used to be their diet. There were ten of them (I had made a special trip in the Land Rover and they had laid six eggs on the way) and they were delighted with their new home. The eldest was called Queen Mary and although she was too old for egg laying, we had brought her to Minack because we did not have the heart to kill her. But the Cornish air, in due course, worked a miracle and she began laying again; and a year later we gave her a set of thirteen eggs to sit on, from which she proudly hatched one chick. Their devotion to each other was pretty to watch until the chick grew into a cockerel and to its duty of ruling the roost; and then Queen Mary, perhaps exhausted by motherhood, began to ail, and had to be put away.

I stood the jug of water on the table and lit the two valor stoves.

The coal stove, in place of the Cornish range, always went out overnight; and so breakfast was cooked with a kettle on one oil stove, a frying pan on the other. Then, while Jeannie got on with the breakfast I walked up to the farm for the milk.

It was not a pretty farm; indeed it was not a single farm but a collection of ancient buildings including three cottages which were allotted to three different farmers. The grey stone buildings were juggled together without any design of convenience for the farmers concerned. A cow-house of one was opposite the tool-shed of another. A barn alongside one cottage belonged to the one opposite. Decrepit buildings, cracked windows, mud and muck on the ground – yet they were a monument to centuries of humble endeavour and this, I found, gave pleasure.

I was looking around for John when an old woman, a

battered grey felt hat pressed down over her ears, with a lined face like that of a Rembrandt portrait shouted: 'He's in the shelter, Mister!' Mary Annie lived with her daughter in one of the cottages, and all her life had been spent among these buildings, working a man's day on the land. She was kind, friendly and happy, and if anyone had suggested she would have been better off in an old people's home she would have laughed in their face. The spirit of Mary Annie was as indestructible as the boulders in the moorland that she could see from her cottage.

I found John sitting on a stool milking a cow. Farmers are silent and solemn people when they are milking, and as they are likely to be performing this task for two hours every morning and evening they have plenty of time for contemplation. Doubtless their thoughts roam over the crops they are growing but I guess they are thinking of those of their neighbours as well. If they do not wish them ill, they at least derive comfort if the crops are not as good as their own. At any rate some of them do; and I confess I developed the habit myself, when our potatoes were 'cut' by frost, of hastening to look at other people's to discover if they were as damaged as our own.

'Lovely morning,' I said cheerfully.

John replied with a nasal sound like 'urr', but without any rolling of the r's. It is a sound with which I have become very familiar. It is uttered by any farmer who does not want to make conversation or commit himself to an answer, and it is emitted on various notes of the scale. If, for instance, a tone of surprise is required, the note is high with a slight cadence. If agreement is to be signified but without it being overstressed the note is in the middle; and if it is necessary to make clear that any conversation is unwelcome, the 'urr' becomes a grunt.

'How are your potatoes looking?' I asked. This enquiry, during growing time, is the Cornishman's substitute for enquiring after anyone's health.

A low 'urr'.

I hung about for half a minute, then asked if I could help myself to the milk and I would pay him at the end of the week. The 'urr' came out in the middle of the scale. Then, as I was going through the door, I heard him say, 'Cubs are makin' a mess of them taties down cliff and I be setting traps.' Fearing for Monty, I was immediately on my guard. 'Whereabouts?' There was a pause. 'They won't harm yer cat,' he answered without me having to explain what I was thinking.

In one direction stretched the lane to the main road, nearly a mile long with its surface straddled with cart-made craters; in the other the lane to Minack, rough like the dried-up bed of a river. Tommy Williams had cut away the undergrowth of the last one hundred yards and we could now drive up to the cottage in the Land Rover. Cars could reach the farm buildings but they could not get any further, and in time the lane became known as our chastity belt. We could not be surprised by visitors and, if tempted to go out, so bad was it even for a Land Rover, we usually had second thoughts about going.

I walked happily down the lane carrying the milk in a tin can, marvelling at the way the hedges on either side unfolded the view of the sea like a tape. First a pin point of blue, then stretched as if it were a few inches long, growing longer and longer as I went down the hill until I reached the bottom and the hedges fell away and I looked upon the vastness of Mount's Bay.

I was singing when I came up to the cottage, breakfast ahead of me, and a lovely day at our mercy. Jeannie was waiting at the door, a jug in her hand.

'You clot,' she said, 'when you filled this jug you filled it with tadpoles.'

*   *   *

The tadpole problem remained until they grew into frogs. I used to crouch beside the stream with a jug and a cup, flicking the tadpoles out of one and emptying the water into the other. It was a laborious way of fetching water, and more so when we needed water at night, and then Jeannie would gleam the torch on the swimming black spots while I repeated my methods of the daytime.

44

We were, in fact, leading the life of two campers, and the prospect of continuing to do so appeared to stretch far ahead. The cottage was sparse of furniture. We had no bed and we slept on a mattress laid on the floor. Our pride was a fitted carpet in the sitting-room but with it we had only one armchair, a divan, a table and three kitchen chairs. We saw no reason to grumble. We had left our furniture behind for the very good reason it was earning us money.

The house at Mortlake which we ourselves rented unfurnished, had been let by us to a young Embassy official and his wife. The profit we derived was to be our income at Minack, and we therefore took care to see that our tenants would be satisfied. He was a solemn young man, and neither he nor his wife had been away from their native land before; and when, after a lengthy inspection of the house they expressed their desire to rent it, I proposed that it first should be vetted by the chief of his department. The chief arrived, inspected and gave his blessing both to the house and the rent; and as the young man wanted to move in as quickly as possible, he and I came to a gentleman's agreement that he could take possession without waiting for the formal agreement to be signed.

Hence, although we were now without furniture we did have a small income . . . but not for long. Three months after the young man had moved in, just as the lease was about to be signed, he moved out. I contacted his chief and also the Embassy concerned, but with no result. A gentleman's agreement was not a valid document. Thus Jeannie and I suddenly had our income cut off, had an empty furnished house on our hands, and were three hundred miles away from superintending its reletting. It was a worrying situation until I said to Jeannie: 'Look, we've been compromising by keeping the house. At the back of our minds we've been thinking we *might* want to go back. We won't and we know it. Let's give it up.'

Early one late summer morning we got out the Land Rover and drove up to London; and by the following day we had seen our landlord, given up the lease and sold him the fittings, and had arranged for some of our furniture to be sold, some to be transported to Minack.

The incident was a warning that escape is not an end to itself and it sharply removed from our minds the pleasant reflection of its achievement. London was no longer our home. It was now vital to make a success of the apprenticeship in the way of life we had chosen to follow; and it is the story of this apprenticeship that I am ready to tell.

4

APRIL passed, the potato season drew near and the inhabitants of the district, including ourselves, began to develop the mood of prospectors in a gold rush.

Three and four times a day Jeannie and I inspected the land which Tommy Williams had planted with one and a half tons of seed – the small meadows he had cut out of the top of the cliff, and the upper part of the cemetery field. The sight fascinated us. We stood and stared at the dark green leaves, hypnotised by their coarse texture, greedily calculating the amount of the harvest; then we would bend down and tickle a plant, stirring the earth round it with our hands, and calling out when we found a tiny potato . . .

'Need a nice shower,' Tommy would say, 'and they'll treble in size within a week.' Or in the lane, I would meet John who, in answer to the inevitable question: 'How are the taties looking?' would say gloomily, 'Been known for a gale to come at this stage . . . blast them black and only the weight of seed been lifted.' It was not only the size of the harvest which was at stake, but also its timing. There was a rivalry among growers as to who would be the first to draw, like jockeys at the starting gate; and the information that was circulated was as inspired as that on a racecourse. I would go up to Jim Grenfell's pub at St Buryan in the evening and listen to the gossip.

'Bill Strick was cut by frost last night.'

'Over at Mousehole they look handsome.'

'Nothing will be going away until after Buryan Feast.'

'William Henry starts drawing Monday.'

These rumours and false alarms increased as the pace of excitement grew faster every day, and by the end of the

month the inevitable question had become: 'Started drawi[ng]
yet?' The disinterested – the postman, the man at the garag[e]
the proprietor of our St Buryan grocers, put the question [as]
a matter of politeness; our fellow grocers, whether neigh[-]
bours or others living a few miles away, jerked it out as if
they were apprehensive we might spring a surprise. Our
land, having never grown potatoes before, might upset the
balance of prestige . . . supposing Tangye was first to draw?
Of course, we caught the fever ourselves and went staring
jealously at meadows other than our own, and asked repeat-
edly: 'Started drawing yet?'

The mounting tension had an effect similar to the concern
of a general who feels he is being pushed into battle before
he is ready. There was the pressure of local prestige on the
one hand, hard economics on the other, and the economics
were very confusing.

Supposing the price on a certain day at the beginning of
the season was 1s. a pound but a week later it dropped to
8d. a pound. In that week the crop may have doubled in size
and you would therefore be receiving 1s. 4d. a pound. On
the other hand the increase in weight would cost more
labour and more in freight, and require twice as many chip
baskets; and in any case the price might have dropped to
6d. a pound and the crop failed to increase as expected.
Moreover for the early potato growers like ourselves whose
crop is grown on the cliffs, there was always the shadow of
the farmers. We had to hand dig our crop with a shovel,
while they careered through their fields with tractors towing spinners. These spinners threw out the potatoes so fast
that with sufficient labour a farmer could send away ten
tons in a day; and so our economic survival depended on
clearing our crops before they began.

There was the bewildering problem of marketing. No
difficulty existed about finding a salesman, the problem was
which salesman to choose. Several had visited us representing different firms and different markets but their methods
of approach were the same; they smiled winningly, talked
jovially, and then offered us identical terms. We had to
pay 9d. for each chip basket (chips were used at the begin-

ing of the season), pay the freight charges and ten per cent ommission on the gross sales, and had to trust to luck for he price obtained on the morning our consignment arrived n the market. With this information I was able to calculate approximately how much each ton of potatoes we sent away would cost us. One hundred and sixty chips were required for a ton – £6. Each chip was scheduled to contain 14 lb of potatoes but another 1 lb was required to allow for shrinkage in transit; if the price, then, was 8d. a pound, we would give away £5. The charge for freight to the Midlands or London (and it had to be passenger train in order to travel overnight) was another £10 a ton. There was paper to put in the chips, string with which to tie them, and the cost of taking them to Penzance station – another £5.

Thus we had to pay £26 a ton, or about 3d. a pound out of the price we received in the market – in addition to the ten per cent commission. Then there was the cost of the seed, fertilisers and labour involved, all of which had to be covered before we made any profit ourselves. From the purist's point of view all new potatoes should be in chips because they travel and keep much better than when they are in sacks; but the 56 lb sacks cost only a shilling, the shrinkage required for each sack is only an extra 2 lb and these are despatched by freight train instead of by passenger train. Hence there would be a stage during the season when potatoes had begun to arrive in the market in bulk with the consequent drop in price, when sacks would replace the chips.

One Monday morning Tommy Williams came striding up the lane while we were sitting on a rock sipping cups of coffee, idly watching Monty stalk a mouse in the grass. Tommy was now working the first three days of the week for us, another two days for John; and thus his loyalty to the potato meadows was divided. On this particular morning he had an evangelist look, his chin thrust out, and his tall figure in ragged working clothes like a prophet on the warpath. 'John's told me he's starting to draw this morning,' he rushed out as if he had brought news that war had been declared, 'we must go down the cliff at once and see what ours are like. You bring the chips and I'll take the shovel.'

We swallowed our coffee and off we went, Tommy with the shovel over his shoulder, I with a bundle of chips, and Jeannie walking hopefully behind. The weather was perfect. The sea was smooth as a pool and flecked with gulls swimming nonchalantly like ducks; and as we trudged down the cliff the old steamship *Scillonian* sailed past outward bound to the Scilly Isles, cutting through the water as gently as a yacht. Tommy brought out the telescope he always carried with him. 'Got a car on board,' he said importantly. In the summer she sailed to and fro to the islands every day, and in the winter every other day in each direction except when the Scilly flower season was at its height. She was a friendly sight and she became, as her successor has also become, a timepiece. 'Has the *Scillonian* gone past?' I would call out, or Tommy or Jeannie.

Her course took her parallel to our meadows a half mile out, a sea green painted hull and a yellow funnel; and sometimes in a storm when the sea was running mountainous waves we would watch with our hearts in our mouths as she lurched toy-sized among them. Then Tommy – brutally – would roar with laughter; 'I bet them passengers are feeling bad.' In fair weather she berthed at Penzance, in bad she made for Newlyn, and as she was the link between the Scilly flower growers and the mainland markets, her skipper sailed her in seas when she might have been expected to remain in harbour. There was one occasion when, after leaving the islands, a gale so fierce blew up that when she reached Mount's Bay she was three hours late and it was dark. The skipper, a Scillonian, unexpectedly decided it was too dangerous to enter Newlyn harbour, and chose to spend the night steaming to and fro across the Bay, sailing out the gale. There was wry laughter in the Scillies when this was known. The Government, a few weeks before, had announced that the Scillonians were to be liable for income tax – and off the boat the following morning stepped two sick-looking Inland Revenue Inspectors.

We reached a meadow at the top of the cliff and I cut the

string of a bundle and singled out a chip while Tommy banged the edge of the shovel on his boot in the manner of an acrobat calling attention to a special trick. Then, with Jeannie and me standing expectantly beside him he stabbed under a plant and turned it upside down. Several little white potatoes connected together as if by a string lay in the soil. Tommy said nothing and moved to another part of the meadow and stabbed again. The same thing happened.

'Looks like we're going to be disappointed,' he murmured, 'we'll try the May Queen over there. They should be ready.' We walked over to the meadow which was steep and fringed with bluebells. Tommy turned over one plant, then another, picked up the stems and shook them, and ran his hands through the soil. We were out of luck. The May Queen were no better than the Pilot we had tried first. 'Marbles!' Tommy snorted with disgust, 'just marbles!' We gathered up the little white things for ourselves, cross and disappointed, and trooped back silently, disconsolately to the cottage. As Tommy put away his shovel he looked at me, his eyes no longer blazing, and grunted: 'Don't say a word to anyone in the village about this. Keep your affairs to yourselves. Some of them are a mean lot and they'll be pleased.' I nodded solemnly in agreement.

* * *

Our village of St Buryan stands on high ground three miles from the coast on the road to Land's End, and the church spire is a beacon to ships far out to sea. It is a sturdy village of neat granite cottages with grey slate roofs and no pretensions about being quaint. It is a business-like village and makes you feel that it prides in brawn and courage rather than in brain and guile, in the basic virtues rather than those which are acquired. Until a year or so ago there was no main water and the village supply was tapped from a spring in the square opposite the inn; so that when you stood in the bar looking out of the window, you watched the inhabitants filling their pails of water as their ancestors had done patiently for centuries before them. It is a village which challenges the sensibilities and yet soothes them, as if it were an integral part of the gales which lash it and the calm which follows. It is not a village in which to live and be idle, for work conscientiously performed is the yardstick of value. It is generous both in spirit and in pocket, for no worthy cause fails to meet with success; but if it is willing to like, it is also quick to distrust, and slow to forgive. It is, in fact, a village of character.

The name comes from that of an Irish girl saint and is pronounced Berian. How she came to the Land's End peninsula is obscure, but in ancient days Irish pilgrims used to travel to the continent by way of Padstow and Mousehole. The object was to avoid the stormy passage around the 'corner' of England by landing at Padstow, travelling overland to Mousehole and embarking in another ship for France. It is believed that in the sixth century she was one of these pilgrims. In any case the shrine of St Buryan existed in the tenth century when King Athelstan swept into Cornwall to drive out the Danes who garrisoned the county and the Isles of Scilly. His final great battle in Cornwall was at Boleigh Hill, two miles from Minack, and he afterwards rested his troops at St Buryan before setting out from the beaches of Sennen near Land's End to invade the Isles of Scilly. On the day before he sailed he worshipped before the shrine and vowed, if the expedition was successful, that he would as a thank-offering build and endow a church.

The original church decayed into rubble in the fifteenth century and at the beginning of the sixteenth the present one was built. It is a beautiful old barn of a building, and in a village whose limited number of inhabitants are divided between Methodists and members of the Church of England, it has the effect of a cathedral. In a corner of the church is a collection of ancient finds that have been made in the district and which were gathered together by a remarkable old man named Croft who was Vicar of St Buryan when we came to Minack. It seemed that Croft was as much interested in the past as he was in his parishioners and he spent much of his time seeking the history of the parish from ancient documents and in leading groups of earnest archaeologists in excavating from the soil the traces of

Stone Age settlements.

A few months after our arrival, a mason repairing a wall in the cottage had discovered a cavity, neatly roofed with small stones, which he explained was an old oven dating back some five hundred years. A few days later I looked out of the window and saw an old man struggling slowly up the steep path to the door. 'The Vicar's come to call!' I cried out to Jeannie, and Jeannie in those few split seconds between the sight of an unexpected visitor and his arrival, rushed round the room picking up papers and hiding unwashed plates. 'Why didn't he warn us?' she moaned, while I wondered how I was going to explain why I never went to his church. I ushered him into the room and he sat down on the sofa, panting from the exertions of his walk. He sat silent until he had recovered himself then, with a gleam of excitement in his eyes, looked at me and said, 'I've come to see the oven.'

The trail of archaeologists used to irk the inhabitants of St Buryan and there was one old man, many years ago, who became a hero to the village for the trick he played on a group. He was a specialist in stories about Athelstan's Battle of Boleigh which, he declared, had been handed down from father to son in his family from generation to generation; and so sincere was his note of authenticity that historians never failed to bring out their notebooks in excited belief. The fields where the battle is supposed to have been fought are known as Gul Reeve which is the old Cornish for 'red field'; and as neither the soil nor anything else in the neighbourhood is red, it has always been presumed that the name is derived from the blood which flowed. Near by is a farm and the old man declared one day to a group of believers that the dead of the battle were buried in a long trench in a field adjacent to the farm buildings. He knew the exact position having carried in his head the number of paces from each corner of the field that led to the trench, details which had been told to him by his father. A score of men dug for two days and not a bone was found. The archaeologists were angry, the men who had done the digging happily pocketed their pay, and the old man grinned. 'If mistake there be,' he said, 'it be due to father.'

On these same Gul Reeve fields stand, some distance apart, two massive upright stones which are known as the Pipers. They are, in fact, Peace Stones, representing the Conqueror and the Conquered, erected presumably after the Battle of Boleigh. But during the centuries in between they acquired the name of the Pipers so that they might dovetail into the story that the elders of St Buryan told their children about the circle of nineteen stones known as the Merry Maidens which stand in a field a few hundred yards away on the other side of the road. The elders told the story as a warning against playing on Sundays. The nineteen stones were nineteen maidens of the parish who were lured by two young men to dance on a Sunday afternoon; and while the girls tripped daintily hand in hand, the young men played their flutes – until there was a flash of lightning and they were all turned to stone.

*　　*　　*

Our post came from St Buryan, and the telegrams from a sub-post office at Lamorna. Our first postman had an eccentric sense of delivery and his route to the cottage across fields and over hedges was to him an unwelcome steeplechase. Letters, therefore, somtimes reached us two days late, sometimes three, sometimes not at all. This waywardness fitted our mood until one morning I received a writ for an unpaid account without ever having seen the letter of warning which preceded it. The telegrams also came across the fields, and the authorities awarded the sub-postmaster with a special bonus of sevenpence for each delivery. Usually they were from Americans who had arrived at the Savoy to find Jeannie had left, and a telegram would arrive asking us to lunch the following day as if the distance between Minack and the Strand was that between Chelsea and Kensington; or else it would be a request for us to telephone at some inconvenient hour as if the charge was a fourpenny call and the call-box in our front garden.

After a sequence of such requests I made enquiries about installing a telephone, half-hearted enquiries which were

56

more of a gesture to conventionality than a desire to have one; and made in the confident belief that the cost of installation with its half mile of wire and poles would in any case be prohibitive. I was surprised when the Post Office informed me that the cost would be twelve shillings and sixpence and the installation immediate; and the Post Office was surprised when it received my letter explaining I had changed my mind and did not want one after all. We still have no telephone and although it is sometimes irritating to drive two miles to the nearest call-box, we are spared the far greater irritation of a menacing ringing bell.

A month after our arrival, and when the tension of the impending potato season was reaching its climax, we received a telegram, 'Expect me tomorrow night' and signed 'Uncle B,' – the nickname by which many knew Baron, the photographer. He was to be our first visitor and the first to pose a problem difficult to solve. If you earn your living from the land you have to work regular hours like anyone who goes to an office, but unlike the office worker, you do not have the security of an office building to shelter you from your friends. A further difficulty is that most people who visit Cornwall are on holiday with time to spare and an inclination to look up old friends or to stay with them for a night or two at the same pressure of gaiety as in the days of their former acquaintance. On our part although we usually quailed at the prospect of visitors, we surrendered when they arrived and suffered penitence for the lost hours after they had departed. Our real difficulty arose when such visitors arrived in sequence throughout a summer, each an old friend regained from the past, each deserving the full attention of a merry reunion. It was on such occasions, and those when we paid rare visits to London, that our ego of sophistication reasserted itself leaving that of the peasant to provide the remorse.

The gusto of Baron was that of a roaring gale which eventually exhausts itself into stillness. He pounded every twenty-four hours like a punchball, working, playing, loving, talking, drinking, dazzling his friends with his wit, kindness and a great gentleness. His behaviour was often outrageous.

He once asked me to introduce him to Mike Cowles, proprietor of the American magazine, *Look*, and I arranged that we should all meet at Claridge's for drinks. After an hour and there was no Baron, Jeannie suddenly turned to me, 'Heavens,' she said, 'it's Thursday!' Thursday was a notoriously unreliable day for Baron as it was the day of his weekly Thursday Club luncheon. Another half hour and we saw him beaming smiles at surprised strangers as he weaved his way towards us. 'Jeannie, Jeannie,' he cried, 'forgive me, forgive me!' And he thereupon knelt down in the dignified foyer, clasping his hands together in mock prayer. A few days later I was with him in the Savoy bar when Mike Cowles passed by and I waved. 'Who's that?' asked Baron. I told him. 'That's the very man I want to meet,' he replied, 'do introduce me.' I put down my drink and looked at him. 'I have done so already . . . we all spent an hour together the other evening at Claridge's!'

Our spare room at Minack was a chicken house which we had bought and converted. We had erected it adjacent to the cottage with its floor lifted clear of the soil by pylons of stones, and the windows looked out on the croft and Mount's Bay. On the floor was a rug, and the furniture consisted of a camp bed and chest of drawers. We had painted the walls white and there was little sign of the hut's original purpose except a small hatch door at ground level where the chickens should have come in and out. Baron was delighted. 'Just the place for an old rooster like me,' he said. He stayed with us on that occasion for twenty-four hours and during that period we visited every pub in the district. We ended the first evening at the Tolcarne in Newlyn where Gracie Thomas rules tough seamen of many nationalities in the manner of a kind headmistress. We had been there ten minutes when I saw Baron was the centre of a group of French fishermen who were roaring with laughter. 'En avance à bateau,' he called out when he caught my eye, and off we all went to the French crabber in the harbour and spent two hours of drinking from a demi-john of wine.

*   *   *

We waved Baron good-bye and felt no nostalgia for the life he represented. We were enjoying a honeymoon with the primitive and tasks that could become monotonous – fetching the water from the stream, filling the paraffin lamp, cooking, cleaning, lighting the stove – possessed the brisk pleasure of the unusual. When I first knew Jeannie she could not even boil potatoes, and the first meal she gave me consisted of cinder-burnt chops due to the fact that she was unaware that frying required fat. She now had a file bulky with recipes and it was not long before she added two more – those for Cornish cream and home-made bread. She collected four pints of milk from the farm, poured it into a bowl and allowed it to settle for a few hours. Then she put the bowl on the edge of the stove where there was a gentle warmth and left it overnight. On the first occasion she tried this out I watched her, as excited as a girl going to a first night, skim off a thick layer of yellowy cream and then, with the confident air of a farmer's wife, serve me with thunder and lightning – treacle and Cornish cream on slices of bread. A few weeks later I had a pain in my side and I said to Jeannie, 'I believe I've got appendicitis.' I was nervous of going to the doctor and put off doing so until the pain or 'feeling' became so persistent that I had no alternative but to make an appointment. As I entered the surgery I visioned the hospital, the operation, the convalescence which would keep me incapacitated throughout the potato season. The doctor examined me and poked my side, then asked, 'Have you been eating a lot of Cornish cream since you came here?' And with his question the pain disappeared.

Jeannie's mother sent the recipe for the bread and it was such a success that we never bought a shop loaf again. She makes four one pound loaves out of three pounds of wholemeal flour and three teaspoonfuls of dried yeast. While the yeast is dissolving in a cup of warm water, she mixes half the flour, a tablespoonful of brown sugar and one of coarse salt in a warmed basin. To this she adds the dissolved yeast, about one and a half pints of warm water, mixes it all into a batter and leaves it on the back of the stove for fifteen

59

minutes. The rest of the flour is then emptied into the mixture and kneaded for five to ten minutes – after which the dough is cut into four sections, put into warmed, greased bread tins and left to rise on the back of the stove until the dough has doubled in size. Finally the tins go into a piping hot oven for about three-quarters of an hour, and the sweet smell of baking fills the room.

My mother had arrived to stay when we dug our first potatoes. She came loaded with gifts for the cottage including dust cloths, saucepans, detergents, a pair of sheets, and a water filter. My mother was never thrusting either with her views or with her presents, and when out of a packing case she produced the water filter, she very softly said, 'I was thinking of the tadpoles, dear.'

It was on the first evening of her stay that she saw the square figure of John leading his horse and cart, piled high with potato chips, past the cottage. She was irritated that he should be meeting with potato success while we were sitting back and waiting, and she urged that we were not showing enough confidence in our meadows. I explained that we had planted our seed later than he had done, that our meadows in potato parlance were considered later than his, and that in any case Tommy had warned us to wait another week. My mother, however, had the gambling instinct inherent within her and she insisted that no harm would be done if I collected the shovel and the three of us went down the cliff to try a few plants.

The bright light of day had gone from the cliff when we reached it and the sun was dipping to the sea on the other side of the Penwith peninsula. The shadows of the rocks were enjoying their brief passage of life before dark, and the sea was dotted with the waking lights of the pilchard fleet. I poised the long-handled shovel and cumbersomely jabbed it under a plant, lifting the bundle of earth and tossing it to where Jeannie was standing. She stooped, shook the sturdy leaves, and ran her hand through the soil. And there, gleaming bright in the dusk were six potatoes, each the comfortable size of a baby's fist.

Jeannie and I were up at dawn the following morning and

I drove the Land Rover over the shoulder of the cemetery field and down to the top of the cliff. It was a heavenly morning with a haze hiding the horizon, the first swallows skimming the landscape, the white parasols of the may trees pluming from the green bracken, and the scent of the bluebells mingling with the salt air of the sea. In the back of the car we had a spring balance weighing machine and a tripod on which to hang it, a bundle of chips and a ball of binder twine with which to tie the cardboard tops when the chips were full, a pair of scissors, the shovel, a box full of salesman's labels with printed addresses of different markets. It was a lush moment of hope blissfully blinded from the realities the years would see.

5

DURING the days that followed, smoothly dressed salesmen appeared on the cliff, watching me dig and ache my way through a meadow, bantering me with news of prices better than their rivals.

'We paid 8½d. home at Bristol,' one would say, and then another two hours later would announce: 'Manchester is strong. We expect 9d. tomorrow.' They served too as the errand boys of news from other potato areas and I would clutter my worries over the prices with the threats that these areas, so much larger than our own, would soon be in production. These threats became progressively worse in their nature, beginning gently with: 'Marazion starts next week,' edging dangerously to 'Gulval are opening up their fields,' or the generalised black news that 'the farmers begin Tuesday': and growing to a climax with 'Jersey are at their peak' or 'Pembroke has a bumper crop,' and then, most disastrous of all: 'Lincoln has begun.' If you have not cleared the cliff by the time Lincoln stream their potato lorries to the markets, you might as well tip your potatoes in the sea. Nowadays these threats have become internationalised and one goes dizzy with the news that Covent Garden is flooded with Morocco, Birmingham with Cyprus, Liverpool with Malta; and it is only when you hear that France has Colorado beetle and has stopped sending that you have a glimmer of hope.

Tommy Williams, during the three days of the week he worked for us, dug in one meadow while I struggled in another; and at the end of the day he would have forty full chips to my fifteen. The Cornish shovel has a long handle like that of a rake and, until one becomes accustomed to it, is a most unwieldy instrument to use. You do not dig as if it were a spade, but scoop under the potato plant using your leg just above the knee as a lever, the left if you are right handed, on which you poise a section of the long handle. As I lunged away my mind rattled with the absurd game of guessing how many potatoes would be under each plant. A meadow of potato plants is seldom uniform, some have squat stems, some thin, some elongated as if they were trying to reach the sky instead of making potatoes among their roots. The ideal plant has a tall firm stem with the shine off the top leaves while the bottom ones are yellow – these are called 'going back' and the fattest, most numerous potatoes should be under them. But, as usual, the dogma of experts was frequently at fault, and I dug plants with squat foliage which had many fine potatoes, some with copy-book stems which had few, and some with green leaves and plenty of shine which had plenty. Sometimes I would be digging a meadow where the crop was light and it seemed to take an age to fill a chip. In another, where the crop was good, the chips seemed to fill on their own and I would shout: 'Lovely samples here, Tommy!'

Tommy's mood varied according to the meadow he was in. If it were large enough for Jeannie to follow behind him, she in blue shorts thrusting her hands in the soil and dropping the very small ones in one chip, the rest in another, and he shirtless in patched brown trousers and wearing a sun-drenched Panama hat, he would treat her to endless dissertations on the problems of the world and his theories on their solution: and from the meadow I was in I would hear the drone of his talk with the gentle voice of Jeannie interrupting every now and again. If he were happy and in a meadow by himself I would suddenly hear the roar of his bass voice, startling the placid cliff with the fragment of a hymn. 'When I start singing in Chapel,' he once told me, 'the congregation stops singing so that they can listen to me solo.' The *Scillonian* was always subjected to close scrutiny. 'Got a tractor on board,' he would say severely, as if it had no right to be there. Or he would spy through his telescope a group in the stern: 'Look to me like Indian students.' And this remark would provide the excuse for a monologue on British policy in India.

Sometimes this telescope annoyed me, for there were days

when it seemed more a part of him than his shovel. 'Every time I look at Tommy,' I would say to Jeannie, 'he's staring out to sea.' And Tommy, unaware of my annoyance, would call out: 'That's a Frenchy coming in,' or 'Never seen that white crabber before,' or, if there was a liner on the horizon, 'That's the *Mauretania* bound for Cherbourg.' His diet came from tins and when Jeannie, sickened by the jellified mess of meat he ate for dinner day after day, offered to warm the tin in the oven, he replied, 'It's proper as it is, thanks very much.' There were occasions when he would work for nothing. 'I know what your expenses are,' he would say to me, 'but I want to break the back of this meadow and I won't charge you.'

He did not seem to be happy working for John. 'Mark my words,' he warned, 'I don't think I'll be with him for long.' And sure enough a couple of weeks later Tommy came raging into the cottage. 'It's all over between me and him,' he shouted, and poured out a torrent of detail which was difficult to follow. From then on he worked for us full time, but the row which parted him from John seemed to irritate. He proceeded to carry on a pin-pricking feud with John, sometimes to my embarrassment. One morning I found him planting a clump of lilies in a piece of ground in front of the cottage. 'Where on earth did you get those from Tommy?' I asked. 'They came from the wood,' he replied without looking up, 'and they belonged to my sister.' Tommy's sister had been married to the man who had the farm before John – and he had been killed in his barn by a falling bale of straw. 'I like to think they are hers.' This same line of reasoning governed a later occasion at the time of the flower season when I saw Tommy climb over our boundary hedge and pick a bunch of wild daffodils on the other side. 'You can't do that,' I shouted. 'Oh, yes, I can,' he shouted back – and then I caught sight of John a little way off, silently watching, his cloth cap on the back of his head, a grass stalk in the corner of his mouth like a pipe. I strolled up the field to him, anxious to disclaim any part in the affair. 'I'm very sorry about this, John,' I said, 'Tommy was over the hedge before I could stop him . . . here,' I began to fumble in my pocket, 'here, you'd better have 1s. 6d. for the bunch.' I held out the money and John, like a magistrate's clerk accepting a fine, thrust it in his pocket. 'As you like,' he said, and then turned away.

Tommy's roughness was balanced by his tenderness for birds and animals, and I have seen his eyes soften in wonderment at the sight of a young robin being fed by its parents. Once I saw him half-way up a tall elm, climbing with one hand while the other held a tiny object. 'A baby owl,' he shouted down at me, 'I won't be a minute before I put it back in its nest. You look at the bottom and you'll see two mice its mother must have brought it during the night.' There was the incident of the fox cubs who chose one of our potato meadows as a playground, gambolling at night among the green plants and crushing flat the leaves and stalks. It was the custom in the neighbourhood when this sort of thing happened for the farmer to set traps; and I have seen of an early May morning four cubs each in a corner of a meadow with a leg caught in a gin. I remember how curious it seemed to me that they did not appear frightened, as if it were still part of the game they had started to play in the night; and they waited there as the sun rose until the farmer, in his own good time, arrived to knock them one by one on the head. We, however, were prepared to leave the playground as it was, losing the potatoes to the cubs, but Tommy, on the other hand, was more practical. 'We can't afford to lose the taties,' said he, 'and we mustn't hurt the cubs. I know a way of persuading the vixen to move them to another earth. You leave it to me.' He never told us what he did though I can guess. In any case the meadow was never used as a playground again.

An hour before Tommy was due to go home, he and I used to begin carrying the chips up the cliff. We carried them one in either hand, a hateful, exhausting, back-breaking task, forgivable when the price was high, but when it began to dip I used to mutter curses, as I climbed, against the city dwellers who had no notion of the endeavour that lay behind the potatoes on their plates. Jeannie and I were too tired to weigh them in the evening, and we would have a meal and go immediately to bed, falling into a revolving kaleidoscope of dreams – potatoes with human faces, crushed haulms served for lunch at the Savoy, the *Scillonian* in the guise of a whale, stinging nettles dancing like a chorus, running a cross-country race on a magic carpet which never moved, Tommy looming out of the sky like Mephistopheles. We awoke as tired as when we went to bed, limbs aching, our minds fogged by our dreams and the prospect of another day of chain gang labour. I would get up and put the kettle on the paraffin stove and when it had boiled replace it with a saucepan for the eggs. Then, breakfast over, we would walk along the path to the top of the cliffs where the chips in neat rows awaited their weighing, and suddenly, as if an icepack had melted miraculously before our eyes, we became aware of the glory of the early morning. We looked down on to the sea, glittering from the sun which rose above the Lizard, spattered with fishing boats hurrying to the Newlyn fish market like office workers scurrying to town. A cuckoo flew past, topping the undergrowth, calling as she went. A cormorant perched on the rock that is called Gazell, its black wings extended, drying them against the softness of the breeze. High in the sky a wood pigeon courted another, clapping its wings, then swooping silently and up again, and another clap as sharp as a pistol shot. Around us bluebells brimmed the green grass and foxgloves pointed to the sky like sentinels. Meadow sweet and may blossom clung the air with their scent. A woodpecker laughed. And the sea, sweeping its cool tranquillity to the horizon, lapped its murmur against the rocks below us. Here was the heightened moment when the early morning, unspoilt like a child, is secure from passing time; and when a human being, sour with man-made pleasures, awakes to the sweet grace of freedom.

I weighed, while Jeannie tied the cardboard tops to the chips with binder twine, and while we worked we worried where we would send them. 'I think Birmingham,' I would say, and then, a few minutes later: 'Of course that Scots salesman did say Bristol was very good.' Jeannie would suggest Covent Garden. 'After all,' she reasoned, 'the West End restaurants surely want Cornish new potatoes and should be ready to pay a decent price.' But a few moments later: 'What about Glasgow – the man with one arm said it topped all the other markets last week.' 'All right,' I would reply, 'We'll send to Glasgow.' There would be a pause while I hooked another chip on to the crook of the spring balance. 'Of course there's all that extra freight to think of,' Jeannie would murmur. 'Oh, hell,' I would answer, 'let's send to Birmingham.' We would pack the chips into the Land Rover, make out the invoice and despatch note, and I would drive to Penzance station. And there, as I waited my turn to unload, doubts would arise again for I would see some farmer of great experience and ask him where he was sending. 'Liverpool – I always send north at this time of the season.'

Our indecision could be blamed on inexperience, but as the years passed the guesswork has continued. Growers despatch their produce to the market, and then, like punters, hope for the best, and storm with irritation when they back the wrong town. There is no way of gauging the see-saw of demand. A salesman said to me once: 'Cardiff is going to be very strong at the beginning of next week. I'll take all that you can dig.' We hired extra labour and sweated through the week-end until we had one ton of potatoes to despatch on Monday and off they went to Cardiff. Three days went by and I received no sales returns – and when sales returns are delayed, it is usually an ominous sign. They came a week later and the price, as by then I had expected, was disastrous. I did not see the salesman again till the end of the season when he appeared at the door to ask for seven chips, the balance of those his firm had sold me and for which I had not paid the price of 9d. each. 'They're broken,' I said truthfully, but grimly, remembering Cardiff, 'Well,' he said, 'you'll have to show them to me, or pay.' That was enough. I burst. Jeannie and I had worked for a month in the manner of peasants of a hundred years ago, and we were exhausted both with potatoes and salesmen. 'Get out of my sight,' I yelled, 'go down the cliff and find them yourself.' I have never seen him again.

There are the same lottery selling methods for flowers. Except on special occasions such as Christmas, Easter and

Mothering Sunday, no one seems to have a clue when flowers will or will not be wanted. I have had a telegram from a salesman at 10 a.m. saying, 'Market is glutted,' and another, two hours later from the same man saying, 'send all you can.' There was one February week when the weather in Cornwall reminded one of the Alps. The St Buryan road was impassable with drift snow, no buses could climb the hill out of Newlyn, and the flowers, of course, were unpickable. Yet we ourselves did have a meadow of Magnificence daffodils growing close to the sea which were bravely coming into flower although the ground was white around them. 'We ought to get five shillings a bunch for these,' I said to Jeannie. We proudly picked, bunched and packed them, two boxes with fifteen bunches in each, and then set about thinking how we were going to get to Penzance. We had been cut off from the main road for five days but, propelled by the excitement of our achievement, we spent five hours digging away a track for the Land Rover; and when we reached the station we were greeted as conquering heroes by the porters. 'Nothing going away at all,' said Owen, who was head porter on the flower train platform, 'nothing at all.' Three days later we received our sales returns and scribbled across the bottom were the words: 'Sorry, it's too cold for the buyers.' The price was sixpence a bunch.

There are, too, the hazards provided by British Railways. I have known a consignment of our potatoes take a week to reach Newcastle by freight train and three days to Bristol. During a period when the price is swiftly falling day by day, such delays mean financial loss for which we can claim no recompense. It is, however, when our flowers are delayed that Jeannie and I are most enraged, and the fury is the more violent because one is impotent to do anything about it. We have pursued the arduous task of growing the flowers, then picked, bunched and admired their exquisite freshness in the packed box – only to learn later that they never reach the market in time for sale. There was the time, on a Tuesday, when we sent forty boxes of Wedgwood iris by the special flower train to Hull. The engine of this train broke down, the truck containing our flowers was put in a siding, and none were sold till the Thursday when a shipload of Guernsey iris swamped the market and brought the Wednesday price of twenty-five shillings a box down to five shillings. Thus we had lost £40 through no fault of our own and, as usual, we could claim no compensation – for British Railways absolve themselves from blame provided the flower boxes reach the station of destination within thirty-six hours of the original arrival time. The fact that the scheduled service has failed to deliver them for the next day's market is immaterial.

Such frustrations, however, lay ahead, for during that first summer we had beginner's luck; and when the potato season was all over and the meadows were strewn with the withering tops of the plants which a month previously had looked so green, with a broken chip lying here and there, an unused sack and the crows poking in the soil among the untidy desolation for the potatoes which had been left behind, we estimated we had made over £200 profit. This figure, minute against the background for a year, inflated our expectations owing to the comparative ease with which it had been gathered. If, with so little land yet under cultivation, with only thirty hundredweight of seed, we could make that sum of money, surely in another year we would have room for four times the seed and make four times as much.

My mother, who had rejoined us for the last week of the potato season, was delighted with these calculations: she had spent most of each day standing in the field holding open the sacks for us to fill, making the professionals smile by her ardour, but saving time and temper for Jeannie and myself who had not yet mastered the knack of tipping a basket without spilling the potatoes. Her gaiety, however, was tempered by increasing concern over our water supply. There had been no rain for a month, the water butt was empty, a pencil-sized trickle was all that was left of the stream, and Jeannie had been forced to discover that soap does not really lather in sea water. My mother, naturally, was unable to adjust herself to the situation, and I used to drive to the village tap at St Buryan, fill up a milk churn I had bought and bring it back for her use. It was inevitable that sooner or later we would have to sink a well, and in view of the drought it seemed best not to waste any time.

'Tommy,' I said one morning, 'we're going to dig a well. What do we do?' Tommy, of course, rejoiced in a question which gave an opportunity for a display of his knowledge and he proceeded to inform me of his personal theory that all spring water in the Land's End peninsula came from Switzerland, that the snow in the Alps melted through the crevices to deep underground, and then slowly crept during the course of hundreds of years across Europe and under the Channel to Cornwall. As often happend, he spiced his imaginative discourse with a practical point. 'You can get a subsidy for sinking a well, I fancy,' and so, at his suggestion, Jeannie and I paid a call at the dingy Penzance offices of the local branch of the Ministry of Agriculture. We had been there once before.

It was shortly before we came to live at Minack and we wanted to seek the advice of the then Agricultural Adviser as to how we should grow potatoes and whether he could arrange for a soil analysis of our land. We were ebullient with enthusiasm and naïve with our questions, but the grizzled-faced man greeted our fervour with: 'We don't want anyone else growing potatoes down here . . . you'll be wasting your time and your money.' Incensed at such a reaction to our zest, I said to Jeannie, 'Come on, let's go, we don't want to spend any more time with this moron.' We went back to Minack and the next morning as we were sipping coffee on a rock outside the door, a neat Homburg-hatted gentleman, dressed in a double breasted black suit and wearing shiny black shoes, suddenly appeared. 'I have come to test your soil,' he said solemnly, in the manner of a doctor who might say, 'Let's hear how your chest sounds.' We were delighted, and as I led the gentleman to a meadow we required tested, I found myself feeling ashamed that I had left the dingy office so abruptly. We came to the chosen meadow and our friend bent down, ran his fingers through the soil, then heaped some into a little canvas bag. 'Oh,' he said, 'this *is* a kindly soil . . . I should say this is a *very* kindly soil.' There was a note in his voice which made me sus-

71

picious, and a few minutes later I asked him how long he had been with the Ministry of Agriculture. He smiled at me blandly. 'Only three days,' he said, 'I've just been transferred from the Ministry of Labour. They change us around a lot, you know.'

I was sceptical when I arrived at the dingy office once again and I was thus prepared for the Alice in Wonderland conversation which followed. 'The Ministry,' said the girl clerk, 'cannot grant a subsidy unless a sample of the water has been passed by the County analyst, and you may not start work on the well until an analysis has been approved.' I looked at her limply. 'How can I have a sample of the water analysed if I have not got the water?' She smiled primly. 'That's what we wondered too.'

Our next step was to find the source of water on our land and this could only be done by a water diviner or dowser. The mysterious gift of dowsing defies scientific explanation and if you are not born with it, it can never be acquired. Its use is of immemorial antiquity, but not until Elizabethan times is there any record of its first practical use in Britain; and then some merchant adventurers finding the Germans using it in the Harz Mountains for the prospecting of minerals, introduced its use into the tin mining industry of Cornwall. Scientific instruments can now, of course, trace minerals underground but they still cannot trace water; and whether you live in a cottage or belong to a great oil company planning a reservoir in the desert, you have to pin your faith on the man who communes with water. But a dowser not only has to possess the instinct to trace water. He has to have the sixth sense to gauge the depth underground of the spring, its strength, and its course within a foot or two. There are many stories of dowsers who had judged wrong, of wells that have been sunk at great expense only to produce no water, and my own particular sixth sense on this occasion warned me that unless we were very careful we too might be unlucky.

Our first dowser charged five guineas and displayed such showmanship that he made us feel like natives witnessing black magic. He was a Londoner who had come to Cornwall a few years before and he had, so he told us, made a lifetime study of water divining. 'I've developed a method,' he said proudly, 'that has made water divining almost scientifically accurate.' We gaped in belief as, opening his suitcase, he produced numerous gaily coloured little flags, and a dozen or so forked hazel sticks. 'Now leave me alone,' he said, 'I need to get in the mood.'

We left him and promptly went inside the cottage to watch from a window; and in a few minutes he rose from his prayer-like position and began to shuffle down the lane, his head bent, his hands holding the hazel stick. Suddenly he stopped, took a flag from his pocket, dropped it and then shuffled on. He stopped again, dropped another flag, then came back to the point where he had started and went off in another direction. It was an hour before he called us to join him, and then he proceeded to give us a lecture as to why, under a pink flag forty feet from the cottage, we would find a spring strong enough to flood St Buryan. 'But how,' asked Jeannie meekly, 'are we to sink a well so near the cottage when there are rocks to dynamite?' 'Ah,' said the man, 'that's not my problem.'

It was not only for this reason that we decided to seek the advice of a second dowser. That evening we were in Jim Grenfell's pub when someone said: 'That fellow may be wrong . . . now the man you want is old John Henry. He's never been wrong in his life and he's nearly seventy . . . he'll find you a spring if anyone can.' I was still cautious and during the following few days I asked other people in the district. 'Oh, yes,' everyone said, 'John Henry is the dowser you're looking for.' The Cornish, like the Irish, are adept at providing those remarks which, they sense, will bolster your personal hopes; and in this case no one wished to tell me that old John had given up regular professional dowsing and that, as he himself later put it: 'I be afraid my sticks have lost their sap.' It was so apparent I wanted our dowsing to be a success that to cast a doubt on my hopes would have been an offence.

The old man had kindly blue eyes wrinkling from his gnarled, weather-beaten face, a character who was so much

73

the countryman that the mind, in his company, was blind to any conversation other than that which concerned the open air. I told him about the other dowser and pointed out the spot where the spring was supposed to be. 'The trouble is,' I said, 'it's so near the cottage that I don't see how we could sink a well.' The old man stared at the soil deep in thought, then pulled his forked hazel twig from his pocket, steadied himself as if he were trying to anchor his feet on the ground, and began to dowse. I looked at Jeannie and smiled. I felt I knew what was going to happen; and a moment later the old man swung round to me crossly. 'Minerals,' he snorted, 'not water.' For the next hour he wandered about while we followed as if we were in the wake of a sleepwalker. Sometimes he would stop and the stick would dip, but never, it seemed, in a way that satisfied him. 'Look,' I would cry out hopefully, 'it's dipping!' But the old man only replied by smiling mysteriously. And then we went up to the crest of the hill above the cottage to a point a few yards from the wire netting of the chicken run. Once again he steadied himself, held out the stick horizontally, gripping it as if he were afraid it might catapult from him. It dipped . . . quickly, strongly as if it were making a smart bow. The old man broke into smiles. 'Here's your spring!' he cried out triumphantly, 'come and feel for yourselves!' I first held the twig by myself and nothing happened; but when he clasped my wrists a power went into that stick as if it were a flake of metal being sucked by a magnet. 'Now there's a strong spring,' said John Henry, 'and you won't have to go more than fourteen or fifteen feet to find it. You can be sure of that.'

Fourteen or fifteen feet. It seemed simple. Jeannie gaily waved good-bye to the old man expecting the water to be gushing into a kitchen sink within a month.

*　　　*　　　*

Within a month – the chickens having been moved to a place of safety – there was a hole in the ground seventeen feet deep, eight feet square, and the bottom was as dry as soil in a drought. Its creators were two miners from the Geevor tin mines at St Just, Jack Tregear and Maurice Thomas, and they were as distressed as we were; while old John hastily called in again by me when the fifteen feet limit was reached, nervously scratched his head and said: 'If you go another foot there's sure to be water.'

It was all very well for him to lure us downwards, but for how long were we to pour money down a hole chasing a spring which might not be there? And yet we had gone so far that the tantalising prospect existed of a spout of water waiting to be released within a few inches of where we might stop. We were, of course, given plenty of advice. 'Ah,' said a neighbour, 'you should have had Visicks the bore-hole drilling people. They reckon you have to bore one hundred feet to get a good supply. They charge thirty shillings a foot, but' – looking lugubriously down our hole – 'they do get results.'

One hundred feet! And here we were at seventeen feet wondering whether to call a halt. The miners had hopd to complete the work within their fortnight's holiday and at their charge of £2 a foot I had expected the well to cost £30. But from the beginning the plans went awry. Instead of being able to dig the first few feet with pick-axe and shovel, the miners came across solid rock within a foot of the surface. Dynamite had to be used and dynamite meant the laborious hammering of the hand drills to make the holes in which to place the charges. Three or four times a day Jack and Maurice would shout 'Fire!' – and scamper a hundred yards to the shelter of a hedge while we ourselves waited anxiously in the cottage for the bangs. One, two, three, four, five, six . . . sometimes a charge would fail to explode and after waiting a few minutes the miners returned to the well to find out the reason; and there was one scaring occasion when Jack, at the bottom of the shaft, lit a fuse which began to burn too quickly. He started scrambling up the sides, pulling himself by the rope which Maurice held at the top. These events added to our distress. The well was a danger besides being a dry one.

I was now paying them by the hour instead of by the foot and the account had reached £50 without value for money except the sight of a splendid hole. It was a hole that taunted us. It laughed at us. It forced us to lean over the top peering down into its depths for hours every day. 'Now let's go and see how our hole's getting on,' Tommy Williams would say as often as he felt I would not mind him dropping the work he was doing. The miners had carved a rectangle and the point where John Henry's stick had dipped was its centre; the sides were sheer, the slabs of granite cut as if by a knife. We would stare downwards and when our eyes had grown accustomed to the dark we would gaze at the veins which coursed between the dynamited rocks; the veins through which, if a spring was near, the water would flow.

The miners would make hopeful comments and Jack would shout up from the depths: 'The rab here feels damp.' By now the hole had become a talking point in the district and monotonously I would be asked, 'Any luck yet?' It became, too, the reason for a walk and in the evening or at the week-end neighbours and far neighbours would lope towards it and add their opinions as to its future. 'Now I reckon you'll have to go thirty feet before you strike water,' said one. 'My cousin Enoch found plenty at twenty,' said another. 'In Sancreed parish,' said a third, 'there are two wells within a mile of each other forty feet deep and never a drop of water from either.' Tommy Williams would comment about these remarks with acid sharpness. 'That fellow,' said he about one who prophesied we were wasting our time, 'is worried about his own water, he's frightened we might drain his.'

We were down twenty feet, then twenty-one, then twenty-five. By now, made frantic by the tortoise pace of the hand-drills, we had hired a compressor and the drills to drive into the rock. It speeded the blasting but there was still no sign of a thimbleful of water. Twenty-six feet. Our money was falling into that hole with the abandon of a backer doubling up on losing favourites; and sooner or later we would have to stop. But when? We now had planks across the top and a winch to pull up the debris after each blast; and back we brought old John Henry to stand on the planks so that we would see again the reaction of his hazel stick. Down it dipped relentlessly, a powerful character staunch to its original opinion. 'If you go another foot . . . ' said John.

It was that evening I met the manager of the Newlyn Quarry to whom I described the nightmare in which we were involved. He was a young, Rugby three-quarter type of man who considered my story as a challenge to himself and his organisation. 'I have some compressor equipment and some new drills I want to try out,' he said with a light in his eye, 'we'll bring them out next week-end and we'll have a helluva bang.' The following Saturday a caravan from Newlyn wormed its way through gates and across fields to within a few yards of the hole. A shiny new compressor with a tractor to power it, the manager and his foreman, two quarry men in snow white overalls and polished black helmets who moved speedily about arranging the equipment with the expectant air of conjurers before a children's party. By Monday, I said to myself, we will have water. By Monday the hole was thirty feet deep and my friend had offered to return the following week-end.

Down the hole the next Saturday went a quarry man, the compressor started up its whining roar, the drill spat like a machine-gun, and the dust began to rise, blanketing the bottom. I hung around with the others bemusedly chatting, dazed like a boxer after a fight. 'When I was a child,' I was saying to the foreman, 'I started to dig my way to Australia . . . '

Suddenly from the murk below us was a shout. 'Water! I've struck water!' We let out a cheer which may have been heard across Mount's Bay and I ran around shaking everyone by the hand like a successful politician after an election. Water! It was as if I had won a football pool. I ran down to the cottage where Jeannie was patiently kneading dough on the kitchen table. 'They've found it!' I cried. 'Water! . . . old John Henry was right!'

But Jeannie was going to wait a year for her bath and her indoor washbasin. For one thing our money had gone down the hole. For another, the water turned out to be a 'weeper' which seeped into the well at a gallon or two an hour. And the third reason was that the rains had come. The water butt was full.

6

MONTY hated the proceedings of the well, and the bangs frightened him into remembering the bombs, flying bombs and rockets which were the companions of his youth; and into remembering the night when, the dust of the ceiling in his fur, he hid terrified in the airing cupboard at Mortlake while Jeannie and I frantically searched the neighbourhood believing he had bolted after a bomb had blown the roof off the house. Thus Jeannie, as soon as the miners shouted 'Fire!' always sat beside him, stroking him, until the bangs were over.

But his contentment, these events apart, was a delight to watch and as the months went by he quietly eased himself into the comfortable ways of a country gentleman. He hunted, slept, ate; then hunted, slept, ate. He never roamed any distance from the cottage, but sometimes he would disappear for hours at a time and we would walk around calling for him in vain. He was, of course, curled up in some grassy haunt of his own and he would reappear wondering what all the fuss was about; and although the reason for our searches was mainly due to the simple curiosity of wanting to discover the whereabouts of his hiding places, we also possessed secret fears for his safety. He was, after all, a London cat and therefore could not be expected to have the intuition of a countryman; and we were prepared to appear thoroughly foolish in any efforts we made to protect him. Our concern was due to three reasons – the fact that the colour of his fur made him look, from a distance, like a fox; rabbit traps; and because we knew that sometimes foxes kill cats. And if, by our behaviour, it looked as if we possessed neurotic imaginations, the future proved our fears were justified.

There was, for instance, the young man with an airgun

whom I saw emerge from our wood and begin to stalk, the airgun at the ready, up the field at the top of which Monty was poised beside a hole in the hedge. 'What are you doing?' I yelled, running towards him; and the young man who, in any case, had no right to be there, halted for a moment, looking in my direction and began to make grimaces as if he were trying to tell me to shut up. Then crouching, he began to move forward again. 'Stop!' I shouted again, 'what the hell are you up to?'

I reached him panting, and he stared oafishly at me. 'Have you any chickens?' he said bellicosely. 'I have . . . but what's that got to do with it? You've no right to be here.' He looked at me with disdain. 'I was doing you a favour. I saw a cub at the top of this field and if it hadn't been for you I could have shot it.' At that moment Monty sauntered down the field towards me. 'A cub?' I said. The young man went red in the face. 'It looked like a cub!'

Monty was given the freedom of the window at night and paradoxically, though our fears for him were bright during the day, they were dulled at night. We were deluded, I suppose, by the convention that cats go out in the dark and that a kind of St Christopher guards them from danger. Then one day a neighbour told us he had found the skeletons of three cats outside a fox's earth not half a mile from the cottage. 'There's a rogue fox about,' he said, 'so you'd better look out for your Monty.' A rogue, by its definition being something which does not pursue normal habits, earns odium for its whole species. Badgers, for instance, are generally supposed to be chicken killers but there is unchallengeable evidence that they are not; it is the rogue badger who has brought them their bad name. So it is with foxes – only the rogues kill cats; but once a rogue gets a taste for cats a district will not be safe until the fox is killed. But even after this warning we did not interfere with Monty's nocturnal wanderings. We were aware of the rebellion we would have to face if we tried to stop him, and so we preferred to take the easy way out and do nothing at all. He was agile, he could climb a tree if attacked and, as he never went far, he could always make a dash for the window.

Then one night Jeannie was woken by a fox barking seemingly just a few yards from the cottage, and this was followed by a figure flying through the window and on to the bed. The following night we were determined he should stay indoors, and we gave him a cinder box and shut the bedroom door; and a battle of character began. He clawed, battered and cried at the door while Jeannie and I, trying to sleep, grimly held to our decision that he should *not* go out. At dawn we surrendered. 'After all,' argued Jeannie, as if cats cannot see in the dark, 'it is light enough for him to see a fox if one is about.' Our bed lay against the wall which contained the window, and the window was so placed that with my head on the pillow I could watch the lamps of the pilchard fleet as it operated in Mount's Bay; while beyond, every few seconds, there was the wink of the Lizard light. Three feet below the window was the rockery garden and the patch of trodden earth on which Monty jumped when he went out on his adventures – one moment he could be on our bed, the next outside.

On the night after our attempt to keep him indoors, he was curled asleep on the bed and the window was open. Jeannie too was asleep and I was dozing, when suddenly through my haziness I heard Monty growl like a dog. Instinctively I put out my hand but he was on the window-sill before I grasped him. I fumbled for the torch and switched it on. 'What's the matter, Monty?' I murmured, 'what's outside?' I leant forward so that I was half out of the window with my torch shining downwards . . . on to the head of a fox. There he was so close to the wall that he was touching it, so large that in the first startled moment I thought he was an Alsatian dog, 'Quick!' I shouted irrationally, 'a fox is after Monty!'

But before Jeannie was aware of what was happening the fox was away, gliding down the lane like a ghost, only pausing a second to look back, its eyes meeting the beam of my torch like two phosphorescent pin-points. Monty was still growling and struggled to free himself from my hold. 'What's happened? What's happened?' Jeannie called sleepily. 'Only this,' I replied, 'Monty has seen for himself why he can never go out again at night.' And he never did unless we accompanied him. As for our method of keeping him in, we had a carpenter make a frame of wire netting which we fixed to the open window at night. Thus we had our fresh air and Monty could continue to sleep on the bed. He was perfectly satisfied.

A dividing line between a townsman and a countryman is the attitude to rabbit traps; a townsman abhors them and a countryman considers them a necessity. Today the gin trap is banned by law and only a specially designed trap can be used legally which fits in the entrance of a rabbit hole and kills the rabbit instantly as soon as it comes out. But since myxomatosis rabbits have changed their habbits and instead of using the burrows they lie out in the undergrowth of the open ground; hence gin traps are still in use, illegal though they may be. Our district is still free of rabbits and we hope we may never see them again; but one day they probably will come back and we may live again the summer nights when, with the background of the murmuring sea, we would lie awake waiting, waiting, for the curdling screams that inevitably would pursue the hours until the trapper arrived to collect his harvest.

And yet I found myself, possessing as I did, the intellect of a townsman and the way of life of a countryman, in a quandary. The rabbits showed no appreciation of our efforts to be nice to them, and they ate our anemones, violets and lettuces with the same abandon as they ate those of our neighbours. We bought hundreds of yards of wire netting, but I found they used it as a rope ladder, climbing up it and into the meadow on the other side; or sometimes I would find a hole in the wire neatly made as if by wire cutters, and then I believed the story I had been told that cliff rabbits had teeth as hard as steel, and the intelligence of monkeys. As a townsman I admired their cleverness, but as a country-man I became infuriated by their destruction of my liveli-hood; and so I reluctantly began to trap.

I used to set the traps at dusk, go round to see them with a torch at midnight, and again soon after dawn. The object of these tactics was, of course, to curtail the sufferings of my victims, but the result was hideous to witness; for the brief period of their pain had not sapped their strength, and when the light of the torch announced my coming they darted crazily this way and that within the circumference of the chain which joined the trap to its anchor in the ground. Each time they rushed to escape, winnowing their terror, the gin bit deeper, while I myself, the amateur executioner, fumbled in my attempts to take a firm hold so that with a jerk I could break their necks. Such incidents, etched into the grotesque by the shadows cast by my torch or turned into a Wagnerian Valhalla in the still soft scent of the dawn, gobbled the zest I had to protect our crops.

Then one night I forgot to set my alarm clock and slept peacefully until within an hour of the time Tommy was due to arrive for his day's work. I jumped with horror from my bed and hurried in my pyjamas to the eight traps I had set the night before. Five were undisturbed, in two others were full-grown rabbits each of which must have struggled hard through the night because their trapped feet were gouged red by the gin's fangs, and in the eighth was a sight I will never forget. By some horrible chance two baby rabbits had been trapped together, and as I approached they were knocking each other as they tried to escape, giving the appearance – had I not known what had happened – that they were playing. I killed them and went silently back to the cottage. 'Jeannie,' I said, without telling her what I had seen, 'Hell to the crops. I'm never going to set a trap again.'

The incident was still vivid in my mind when a week later, as we were finishing supper, we heard the tap, tap, tap of the trapper's hammer in John's field above the cottage which ran towards the sea. It was a May evening and although John and I were still on speaking terms, there was a simmering friction between us that seemed certain sooner or later to erupt. 'I do think he might have warned us,' I grumbled, 'we might easily have been out for the evening and then what would have happened to Monty?'

The custom of a trapper was to ring a field with traps two or three days running, leaving them open during the day and setting them afresh in the late afternoon or early evening. Sometimes, however, a trapper was not so conscientious and I remember an occasion when traps on neighbouring land were set at midday on Sunday and were not visited again until breakfast time on Monday. I was waiting when the trapper came down the lane in his car.

'Good morning,' I said, and then without wasting any time: 'I believe you went to Church yesterday evening.' The man looked at me doubtfully. 'I went to Chapel . . . I'm a Chapel man.' 'Well wherever you went,' I replied, my voice rising, 'your aim was to give thanks to God and yet . . . at that very time you were allowing His creatures to suffer agony at your hands.' The man stared at the ground. 'Come here,' I ordered, and led him to a rabbit which was hanging head downwards from a trap set on top of a hedge. 'That rabbit was caught at one o'clock yesterday afternoon,' I said, 'and had I not heard its cry it would have taken several hours to die in agony . . . and you were in Chapel!' My anger, of course, made me pompous but it had an effect. A few months later I saw the man again. He had given up trapping.

Passion, therefore, was always waiting to come to the surface when traps were set – that of Jeannie was born of imagination, mine of experience. And so when we heard the tap of the hammer in John's field there was the growl of anger within us, the dread of the coming night with its screams, the nag of knowing Monty was in danger. On the second evening, a couple of hours before sunset, Monty was sitting in the front garden, sphinx like, eyes half closed, his burnished fur glossy in the light of the ending day. There was no hint he aimed to wander. His white whiskers sprayed his lion cub head, his tail curled round his body so that its tip gently flicked his front paw. He was at peace, utterly secure in the small world we had found for him. Then I looked through the open door and he was not there.

'Where's Monty? He was outside five minutes ago.' We had panicked often enough before, and been calmed, and made ourselves feel foolish that love should exaggerate fear; and yet the instant of warning repeated itself each time with the same spasm of fright. I ran up to the field and stood on a bank.

The young green corn was brushing the soil, and far out to sea aslant to the Lizard a liner was making for Cherbourg. A raven grunted overhead, flying heavily westward towards the sun, and a charm of goldfinches fluttered chirruping before me, then dived out of sight behind the hedge on my right. A buzzard lazily glided, and silent in the heavens a jet traced its plume. It was very still and only the sea whispered. Suddenly across the field a hundred yards away near the gap pencilled by barbed wire which led to John's cliff, I saw Monty's tail flapping in prisoned puzzlement, as if a hand at ground level was feebly motioning a welcome. 'Jeannie,' I shouted, 'Monty is in a trap!'

I led the way across the field yelling: 'Monty, we're coming!' . . . absurdly frightened, my mind racing with stories of trapped cats. 'It's easier to kill 'em,' a trapper once told us, 'than to get 'em out of a trap. That wild they be.' And I felt enraged that a threat guarded against had yet materialised, that even with all our care Monty could still be trapped. Irrational thoughts, I know, but such are often the companions of distress.

He was lying quietly on his side, his little front paw with the white smudge on its squeezed in the gin; and his yellow eyes gazing up at me as if my presence alone was enough to make him believe the trap would release him. Then, when in those first few seconds I did nothing, he uttered a little cry, a querulous cry as if he were cross.

'You'll hold him firmer than I can,' Jeannie said when she reached us, 'I know how to open the trap.' I grasped his soft body, limp as a fur stole, while Jeannie, her knees in the green corn, put her hands on the gin. It would not budge. 'It's rusty,' I said, 'look, it's coated with rust.'

It was as if Monty understood the significance of my remark because he began to cry and struggle and scratch, and try to bite his paw free. 'Hold him! For goodness sake hold him or he'll pull his paw apart!' At that instant he slipped from my hands, lashed out with his three free legs, tugging at the trap with his fourth, claws like knives ready to rip anything within reach. There was blood on Jeannie's wrist.

'Something's wrong with the trap and we'd better get him back to the cottage.' I had the crazy idea that once there I could rush up to the farm for help. 'Pull the peg out of the ground,' I said, 'then take the weight of the trap with the chain while I hold him.' He had become exhausted and was still again, except for his panting which made his body heave like bellows.

We began to walk, a miserable trio, across the field . . . Jeannie with the chain, I holding him in front of me like a tray, the paw and the gin between us.

'What about your wrist?'

'It's only a scratch. Nothing deep.'

We were nearly there. The lump of the chimney bulged at eye level, the height of the field parallel with the roof, the open door now below us waiting. Suddenly Monty gave a twist with such vicious strength that he caught me unawares. He slipped from my hold, and like a macabre juggler I went this way and that in an effort to regain him. 'Keep the chain up!' Miraculously Jeannie succeeded so that the weight of the gin went along with his paw. He had his terror and pain but she saved him from the awful wrench of the weight, and in those few seconds of success I had grasped him firmly again and he was still and limp in my hands.

'I'm going to put him on the ground.' His little pink tongue frothed as he panted and sweat damped his fur and he lay on his side so quietly that he might have been asleep. The next instant I seized the trap, gave it the wrench of a maniac – and it opened. He stretched in the green corn for a minute shuddering with exhaustion; and then Jeannie picked him up and gently carried him home.

Our sweet relief very soon turned into unreasonable anger. Unreasonable because it was nothing to do with us what people did on land under their control. Unreasonable because we had learnt to our cost that rabbits steal with the same effect as a thief putting his hand in the till. Unreasonable because trapping, however much we might disapprove, was the main method of checking the rabbit plague,

Our tempers, however, were flaring and only action could bring abatement.

'I'm going to throw that horrible trap in the sea!' Jeannie had bandaged her arm and Monty was still lying exhausted on the sofa.

'All right,' I said, 'and I'm going to find John.' I tramped up across the fields to the farm and the breeze cooled me and told me to be calm – Monty was safe and there was no point in adding to distress. And then I thought of the scratch on Jeannie's arm, and Monty's panting little body and the sound of the screams of the rabbits at night – and when I reached the farmhouse door I was angry again.

Only John's wife was there, peeling potatoes in the kitchen, and his small son who eyed me silently, suspiciously from a chair by the window as I told my story. 'I know nothing about it, Mr Tangye,' said John's wife, 'nothing at all. You speak to John about it.'

I returned to the cottage to find Jeannie had completed her mission. 'I didn't throw it in the sea,' she said doubtfully, 'I threw it over the hedge into the brush . . . we can always get it back if we *have* to.' My own interview had damped my temper, and I was now wishing it had never taken place. I had fired a shot without the compensation of seeing it land on the target – and John was warned. I was now in any case not sure of my ground; and it seemed to me on reflection that inner forces were at work within us to use the incident as a tilt at John and the attitude he represented. If we were desiring a peaceful life and to be left on our own, this was not the way to go about it. I awaited John's coming.

He came thundering up the lane soon after breakfast the following morning. Cap askew, his face red as a beetroot, squat and powerful as a gorilla, he advanced on me with arms swinging as if his intention was to knock me down. 'What right had the cat to be on my land?' he shouted at me when he was still twenty yards off. 'What right had you to trespass on my land to let him out?'

He was now ten yards away.

'What right had Mrs Tangye to throw my trap away?'

He was now five yards away and he had scored a point.

'I tell you what, mate,' and he had now stopped, thrusting his face at mine, 'from now on you go your way, I go mine. When I come down here I won't speak to you,'

He swung round and stamped away.

7

THE winds curl Minack in winter. In the beginning while we sat snug in the cottage a sense of security acted as a narcotic against the roar outside. A book, a pipe, the scent of a wood fire, Monty on my lap, there was comfort in joining the ghosts who had listened to the same rage, in sheltering within the walls that withstood centuries of siege. Then as we passed through the shoals of first enthusiasm, facing the reality of the task we had undertaken, tension replaced comfort as the winds blew.

I am afraid now when the westerly comes galloping over the hill behind the cottage and charges with thundering hoofs into the elms that edge the wood; when the northerly steps aloofly along the valley, chilling its visit with frost; when the easterly bites from the Lizard, mouthing the sea and ripping our cliff which puts up a hand to stop it; when the southerly brings the rain and the storm which binds the sea and the land in gloom. For all are our enemies. Those from the east and the south carry salt as they blow, salt which films over flower petals and leaves and burns them papery white. That from the west savages the crops like a madman, that from the north shivers black the plants in its way. I have learnt now the wisdom of Tommy's advice when, at the start, he said to me one day: 'We'll have to have good hedges if we're going to save our crops, and the sooner we start planting them the better.'

I remember at the time that I was grateful to Tommy for looking ahead. The evening before, a man in a pub had asked whether we had yet packed our bags. 'Everyone roundabouts,' said he facetiously, 'is sure you'll never stay. You won't stand Minack in winter . . . oh no! Minack's all right in summer. But winter . . . !' Only the seasons could prove to those who were watching us that we were not flirting with the life we had chosen, and that we belonged to the land they loved; like recruits to a battle-proved battalion we had to wait to earn respect. Meanwhile our ways were sure to be smiled at, and our failures seized upon as evidence of coming surrender; and so when Tommy countered the prophecies of our departure by discussing the planning of hedges for the future, his unconscious gesture gave us unreasonable pleasure. But the advice itself made me apprehensive.

There were so many other tasks to perform, so many other things on which to spend our limited capital that it seemed a dreary prospect to lay out time and money on hedges which would take years before they became effective. I know now that my attitude was that of an amateur who is unable to believe that the conquest of the land is only achieved by monumental patience. I was in a hurry. My chief concern was to earn sufficient money from immediate crops to secure our survival. I had no time for the laying of foundations and my faith depended on the years ahead looking after themselves; and yet my instinct conflicted with my inclination and I knew that I should listen to Tommy. 'All right,' I said to him half-heartedly, 'I'll find out what we ought to do.' I proceeded to find out, then discarded my findings, and compromised with a plan of my own; and the result is that even today I am ashamed of my hedges.

Hedge planning is in effect the mapping of a market garden, and that was another reason why I was shy of it. What kind of a map did I want? I did not know. I was not a man sitting at a desk drawing up a blueprint with skilled experience behind him. I could see no further ahead of me than potatoes and more potatoes, interspersed with daffodils, violets and anemones, and I possessed a sublime faith that a vague number of these would provide our living. What number, I had no idea. Nor the ground space which would represent an economic unit. Costs in relation to turnover were a mystery to me and thus prospective profits, if any, were a blank figure. True I tried to find out, but the growers I talked to were loquacious about their contradictory methods of growing yet dumb on finance. They looked prosperous in their fashion and I was not to know that at this particular time they had passed the peak of the war and post-war years and their profits had begun a diminishing side. The Horticultural Advisory Service of the Ministry of Agriculture were helpful on the techniques of growing but they too were silent on how to make a market garden pay. I suppose I was expecting too much of them because Minack, in the eyes of an expert, was a folly, and no professional market gardener would ever consider embarking on the task Jeannie and I had set ourselves. We were aiming to make a market garden out of a home, instead of a home out of a market garden.

It was a coincidence that the Ministry of Agriculture itself was establishing a vast experimental horticultural station from one hundred acres of farm land thirty miles away at Camborne at the same time as we were scratching our heads over our own few acres. Rosewarne, as it is called, is now a showplace of planning achievement and there is not an aspect of horticulture – except how to make it pay – that is not investigated. Similar experimental stations, including those maintained by large private firms, exist all over the country, and in the past few years they have developed into being an industry within an industry. Vast sums of money are spent, hordes of scientists and manual workers employed, bevies of reports are issued – while the humble grower who provides the purpose for all this effort remains in the earthy reality of shortage of capital, higher costs and falling prices.

Progress is the scientist's justification, and in the horticultural sphere this means the conquest of the soil and plant diseases, and the production of larger and better crops. This praiseworthy aim is pursued without any thought of likely economic results and thus a scientist's howl of succes may be the grower's toll of doom. Daffodil bulbs have in the past been checked from over-production by the fly which lays its eggs within them in the spring, the larvae of which eats and destroys them. Today there is a chemical which, if the bulbs are dipped in it before planting, will secure them from fly attack for at least two years; and this is resulting in a staggering increase of daffodils for sale in a market which is already overloaded. Glasshouse lettuce, unless very skilfully grown, has in the past suffered much from boytrytis, a fungus which rots the leaves and stem; now a dust has been produced which can result in a 100 per cent cut of a crop instead of, perhaps, 70 per cent. Rosewarne, among its other activities, is engaged on the conquest of downy mildew on anemones, a disease which attacks large quantities of plants every season and which prevents anemones, as a precautionary measure, being grown in the same ground more than once in every seven years. From the scientist's point of view this would be a conquest worth achieving and hence a mammoth effort is being made to do so; but here again a victory for the scientist means a bell tolling for the grower. 'You know,' said a backroom boy to me gleefully, 'when we succeed . . . anemones won't be worth growing in Cornwall, they'll be so easy!'

Of course, the claims of the scientists do not always prosper in practice, and this adds to the grower's bewilderment. The trade papers bellow with wares of hybrid names promising myself and my colleagues a grower's paradise, luring us to buy concoctions that are found wanting within the year, leaving us with half-filled tins. During the battle of the bulb fly the scientists produced a smelly dust which, they assured us in extravagant language, would kill the menace if dusted over the bulb meadows at fortnightly intervals during April and May, making five applications in all. I bought the dust together with an expensive dusting machine which hitched weightily on my back and was operated by my hand pumping a lever, energetically as if I were a boxer pommeling an opponent. April and May was potato time so I had to be up at dawn marching over the dew filled meadows with the smelly dust spoiling the sweet scented air, exhausted by the energy involved and in any case sceptical whether the effort would be worth the result. It was not. I conscientiously performed my duties for two seasons, then discovered the whole idea had been discarded as worthless by the scientists, leaving me with memories of ruined early mornings, a dusting machine which is now rusted with disuse, and a sack of the smelly dust which seems too expensive to throw away.

Growers, like punters, are gullible and are only too anxious to believe that these dangling promises will provide the profits which are so elusive; hence the chain of scientists, manufacturers and horticultural merchants exercise the same hypnotism as Littlewoods. One autumn I decided to grow spring onions and I had gone through the preliminaries of preparing the ground and sowing the expensive seed when I was advised to use a pre-emergence weed killer. This tempting concoction would spare me the task of weeding throughout the winter and assure a bumper crop at harvest time; and all I had to do, so I was told, was to spray the ground a couple of days before the spring onions were likely to emerge. The timing was important and so was the weather. By leaving the spraying to the last possible moment, I would kill the maximum number of weed seedlings which had grown faster than the spring onions; on the other hand, according to my directions, the weather had to be dry and the sun hot – as if I were able to arrange these factors as easily as opening the weed killer tin. I scratched the ground daily until I saw the seeds had germinated, then looked up at the sky, decided it was going to be fine, and brought out the sprayer. Unfortunately the weather took no heed of the manufacturer's directions and within a few hours there was a sharp heavy shower; and the spray instead of staying on the surface was washed into the ground – and that was the end of my spring onions.

Some sprays are so dangerous that the operator must wear a spaceman's suit when using them. Some, drifting on the wind from a neighbour's field, creep through the open windows of greenhouses and destroy the tomato plants. I have used a spray to kill greenfly on lettuce, and have killed both the lettuce and the greenfly. A spray to kill aphis on brussel sprouts was being spread from an aeroplane when some of it wafted into a country lane bordered with blackberries – police set up road blocks at each end of the lane while the blackberry bushes were forthwith cut down, carted away and burnt. I have never used slug pellets since a friend's dog, finding them scattered in his garden, ate them as if they were biscuits, and died. One season we had a plague of mice eating the anemone buds and, bemoaning the fact to a merchant, I was recommended a liquid which, when sprayed on the ground, killed the mice when they walked on it. 'What about other animals?' I asked, 'cats or dogs, I mean.' 'Oh them,' said the merchant, as if nothing else mattered so long as the mice were killed, 'it wouldn't do them any good either.'

A time came when we had a greenhouse at Minack and the first crop we grew were April sweet peas which had to be dusted with a special powder throughout the winter as a protection against mildew. Sweet pea plants need endless attention, and during the countless days we spent in the greenhouse Monty used to be our companion. We were amused by his presence and innocent that he ran any risk; and indeed we considered the greenhouse his playground so that when the weather was stormy we put him inside so that he could exercise in comfort. One March day we had driven over to Newquay and did not return until seven in the evening when, as so often happened, the tiger-like face of Monty staring from the bedroom window welcomed the lights of the car as we came up the lane to the cottage.

Inside we gave him the usual vociferous greeting and Jeannie, anxious to appease the long absence, doled out the boiled fish on his plate. He made to go towards it, halted, began to stagger, then fell down. Jeannie's back was turned and I alone was the witness. 'Jeannie!' I shouted as if I were calling against the wind, 'what's happened to Monty? He's had a stroke!' Panic can easily seize me and as quickly be defeated, just as my temper can flare and fade. Here seemed the threatened instant of finality, the wink of the eyelid that makes the past unreal, love silenced, the agony of leaning on memories threaded like gossamer. And then, quite suddenly, I was calm again. Monty had got to his feet and was weaving towards the bedroom door, crying, and I bent down to hold him, then picked him up in my arms and saw that

his eyes were glazed, unseeing and circling in their sockets, control abandoned. 'I'll get the vet,' I said firmly, 'if he's in he'll be here inside the hour. I'll get the Land Rover out and go up to the farm and telephone. I'll put Monty on the bed and you do what you can to keep him quiet.'

Within the hour the vet was leaning over Monty, sounding him, taking his temperature, talking to him in a quiet Scots accent, and by his presence alone making us feel the worst was over. 'His heart's sound,' he said, puzzled, 'and I don't see any sign that he's had a stroke and yet . . . ' I suddenly thought of the sweet peas and the mildew powder, and I ran out to fetch the tin. There was no mention of poison on the label but when the vet read the anaylsis he put out his hand and stroked Monty. 'Here's the trouble, old chap,' he said, 'you've been going into the greenhouse and the dust has been brushing off the plants into your fur, and after all these months you've absorbed it into your body. You've got a bad dose of slow poisoning . . . that's what's wrong with you!'

The treatment was bicarbonate of soda every four hours for the next forty-eight and Jeannie and I took it in turns to watch through the night. On the second night, it was shortly before dawn, Jeannie, who was in charge of the difficult task of emptying the spoonful of bicarbonate down his throat, was just about to go off to sleep after giving him his dose, leaving me awake in a chair beside him, when there was a noise from the bed on which Monty was lying. We looked at each other. The crisis was over. The noise from the bed was a purr.

I am, then, suspicious of those who feed from the struggles of growers. Conventionality provides them with a mask of altruism towards us, but it is a thin mask. So vast is the industry that now exists on the perimeter of the once basic one of growing, so many are the ramifications of subsidised bodies that thrive on horticultural research, so huge is the number of men and women whose salaries depend on these sources, that the role of the grower has become that of the guinea pig – the purpose of his existence belongs to others.

I once pinned one of these highly paid gentleman in a corner in an effort to extract from him a practical programme for a mythical market garden. He was well qualified to give me the advice and I had a simpleton's belief that he would provide an answer. 'Supposing,' I said earnestly, 'you were offered £5,000 on condition you gave up your job and spent it on planning a market garden in Cornwall. How would you set about it?' The man looked at me in astonishment, then roared with laughter. 'Good heavens,' he said, 'I'd forget the condition and put the money in Consols!'

Of course, like all who are prejudiced, I am being unfair, expecting too much, forgetting the occasions when those whom I attack have helped. I rely, for instance, on John Davies, Horticultural Advisory Officer for West Cornwall in the same way that in the old days one relied on the family doctor. If a plant shows signs of a mystery disease, if I want soil samples taken, if I want bulbs tested for eel-worm or basal rot, if I just want him to walk round Minack and to listen to his comments, then John Davies will be at my service. And Rosewarne has helped me personally, though it seems to me the expenditure lavished on it far outweighs its usefulness to the ordinary grower.

It is like a wonderful department store where none of the goods are for sale; packing sheds, bulb stores, machinery buildings, heave into the sky like jet liner hangars; an elaborate oil heating apparatus pipes heat to the greenhouses and offices; pedigree cattle and pigs are kept solely for the manure they produce; tractors of the latest design fuss over the land, labourers swarm like bees where mechanisation is impotent; dutch lights and cloches of various shapes and sizes cover an area like a frozen lake. The whole is laid out with the vision of a Capability Brown – avenues and cross sections, myriads of plots where groups of similar flowers or vegetables are grown under different conditions, their progress of growth meticulously noted. It is a vast laboratory, like the site of a space rocket where no expense is spared yet it would be a shambles without a master mind of organisation. One is envious. One feels if one could hitch a particle of the skill and money expended to one's own particular programme, the cares would dissipate. I look at the hedges, thousands of yards of them running sturdy and thick across the open land and marvel at the shelter belts of trees now twenty feet high; and then I come home and stare at the wispy things which represent our hedges, the long gaps between them, the trees which have remained obstinately stunted, tangible evidence of disappointment.

I can plead the excuse of expense. I found that escallonia, the type of hedge planted at Rosewarne, cost £160 for every thousand eighteen-inch plants, that other suitable hedge varieties were around the same price; and so, as I was unable to afford rooted plants I had to use my initiative to take their place. There were already around Minack patches of elder and privet, and at my old home of Glendorgal there were hedgerows of tamarisk. All three stand up to salt winds but, compared to escallonia, they have disadvantages; privet sucks the ground of its goodness and nothing will grow satisfactorily within a few feet of it; elder, when full grown, is often attacked by woodworm and decays into a petrified hedge; while tamarisk usually leaves an unwelcome gap of two feet, through which the wind rushes, before the feathery foliage branches out. But they were free. That was the point which appealed to us, and we gaily treated the difference between cuttings and rooted plants as of no importance whatsoever.

I asked for advice and the advice I received was of the kind I wanted to hear. 'Just stick 'em in the ground,' said an old gardener, 'no need to concern yourself. They'll take.' Tommy, too, was our ally, and for an encouraging reason; he had pushed elder branches into the ground where, the year before, he had dug the meadows in the cliff and now each was a vigorous little plant of its own. It seemed, therefore, that success was limited to the labour involved, and so we proceeded to collect a load of tamarisk branches from Glendorgal, and added hundreds of privet and elder from Minack. It was autumn. It took a week to stick them in the ground, and the winter to find that only a hundred or so had taken. Rabbits were partly to blame for they used the thin cuttings to test out their teeth, nipping them neatly like secateurs, even ignoring the stinking paste I smeared on the bark to check them. Yet the cuttings which escaped their interest fared no better and when in the spring, in irritation, I began pulling them up to see what had happened, the few inches that had been stuck in the soil were as dead as a walking stick. 'Let's put some more in now,' said Tommy, 'they might grow on through the summer.'

We painstakingly collected a further pile of cuttings and once more laboriously stuck them in the ground; and as a gesture to conventional methods I bought a hundred rooted plants called New Zealand Ollearia. Our defeat, on this occasion, was caused by a hot, dry summer; there was not enough moisture to excite the cuttings nor to satisfy the Ollearia, and when autumn came round again the Ollearia had been cut by half and the cuttings had gone the way of the winter ones.

I was beginning to lose patience. At this point, however, I learnt of a chemical solution in which the cuttings could be soaked, which would hasten the growth of the roots. I decided to give it a chance, and off we went collecting cuttings again. We tied them in bundles, dropped them in the tin bath specially bought for the purpose, and waited the required time for the chemical solution to perform its magic. Then, instead of sticking the cuttings haphazardly in an embryo hedge, we arranged them a few inches apart in a meadow. Now, I said to myself, I have at last done the right thing and by the spring we will have several hundred rooted cuttings to transplant. Unfortunately it was the coldest Cornish winter of the century and for a month the ground was frozen like cement. None of the cuttings survived.

This tale of misfortune, I now realise, need not have happened had I been more methodical. The soil does not accept impatience, short cuts, or the attitude of take it or leave it; and it rewards only the careful. The weather is a market gardener's standby excuse but it also covers a multitude of his sins. Hedge plants, like roses, need weeding and watering and the fact that there may be hundreds of them does not hide this necessity. I now know that it is my fault that hedges do not ring Minack. They bored me. There were so many other things to do. They grew too slowly to capture my imagination; and once I stuck them in the ground I forgot them. They could look after themselves.

Jeannie spent the first winter locked in the chicken house we used as a spare bedroom, writing 'Meet Me At The Savoy.' There was the camp bed used by her father in the 1914 war and now strewn with her papers, the rug, a second-hand kitchen table with her typewriter, an upturned box as a chair, another box where a paraffin lamp hissed at night, except when the winds blew and then it was silent against the roar outside. 'Where's Jeannie?' some friends who had called would ask. 'In the chicken house,' I would answer, 'here's the key. Go and see if she wants to be let out.'

This apparent brutality, I say in self defence, was at her suggestion because she was aware that incarceration was the shortest way to completing her book. She had no one to help her in the cottage, and though it was small and though I did what I could, the eyes of a woman saw work to do; and so if she had freedom of movement the mind would fuss and time be wasted. Thus I would clean and light the stove, make a gesture of dusting the two rooms, do the shopping, provide a snack lunch and endless cups of tea; and then in the evening Jeannie would emerge to cook the dinner.

She performed this tiresome task quite unconcerned that the world she had left on her typewriter was a gay and glamorous one, while reality was that of a peasant. The essence of marriage is ease of companionship and this the two of us shared. Our professions had forced us to mix with people as a duty, and it was a duty which we often enjoyed; but neither of us were ever dependent on mass companionship, the sickness of being afraid of being alone. And now that time was ours we saw no virtue in leaning on conventionality; attending gatherings whose purpose was to hide the boredom of those who gave them. We kept to ourselves. We did not have to escape to pleasure, for pleasure was watching Monty jumping Monty's Leap or noting the time the woodpecker went to bed in the hole of an elm twenty yards from the cottage, or wondering what bird called a piping cry at dusk, or opening a parcel from the London Library, or becoming aware of the colours of lichen, or that of old stones, or rejoicing that we were both so lucky. We would have dinner with the candlelight flickering the white walls, and discuss what she had written and what she planned to write on the morrow, and I would give an account of what I had been doing during the day. And then we would clear the table and cover it with newspaper, for there was still work to do.

Violets waited to be bunched.

8

WE had planted the violet runners in June – six thousand
Governor Herrick in the top half of the field, the cemetery
field where we had cropped potatoes; and two thousand
Princess of Wales in the meadow walled by elms near the
cottage which we whimsically called 'Gee's Meadow' at the
request of Gertrude Lawrence. 'It would give me a nice
warm feeling,' she wrote to us from New York, 'if I knew
there was a corner of England which was for ever me.'
Sentimental, loyal, enchanting, provocative Gertie – what
compelling force made me go into that meadow one
August evening and be quietly standing there when Jeannie
came running, calling: 'Gee's dead! . . . a cable from
Richard . . . !'

Death can bring anger as well as grief. The old die creeping gently into our sorrow but those with uncompleted
lives, promise unfulfilled, gifts unspent, savage the placid
sweetness of our memories, thrusting frustrated yearnings
into our hands, bruising the tears with cries of what might
have been. 'Rage, rage against the dying of the sun!' said
Dylan Thomas.

Gertie's life – or Gee or Gertrude – although she herself preferred Gee, belonged to the age when talent of the
arts was leisurely matured so that the future was always
more enrichening than the past. Time hovered instead of
rushing, yielding the opportunity to delve into the secret
self, extracting from its recesses the uncorrupted truth.
Temptation was not always at the elbow to offer the illusion
that sudden fame was permanent success because the arbi-
ters of achievement – the Charlots and the Cochrans – were
governed by standards that did not admit false values. Thus
Gertie, steered in her youth by their guidance, was able to

find as she grew older the gifts deep within her which earned the homage that dipped the lights of Broadway and Shaftesbury Avenue on the August evening that she died.

Gertie had an irrepressible ebullience which enabled the sleek or the humble to rejoice in her company – an audience of 'Private Lives' or that of troops in a concert hall. She had no conceit and beneath the gloss was a perennial wonderment that the little girl who once danced to the barrel organ outside Kensington Oval had become a star in two continents. She preferred to remember her childhood rather than to forget it, and this was the strength of her sympathy for those who were struggling. Danny Kaye made his début on Broadway in 'Lady in the Dark' of which Gertie was the star, and on the first night he brought down the house with a song he sang just before her own big number. Danny, instead of being delighted, was terrified. How would Gertie react? He could not believe that she would be pleased – but of course she was and insisted that he be promoted to star billing. A few years later Danny came to London to repeat his first big triumph at the Palladium, and at the same time Gertie had a great success in Daphne du Maurier's 'September Tide'.

'How's Gee?' he asked Jeannie on the morning of his first night. Jeannie replied that she thought she was rather lonely. 'You see,' Jeannie said to Danny, 'here she is with London at her feet but she is so famous and glamorous that people hesitate to ask her out thinking she would never come anyway, and the result is she often gets left out.' Danny picked up the telephone and asked for Gertie's room. Jeannie heard her tinkling voice reply, then Danny saying: 'Will you be my girl tonight, Gee? The American Ambassador is giving a party after the show.' And there was another day when Danny came rushing into Jeannie's office. 'Do you know what day it is?' 'Yes, of course,' she answered, 'it's Independence Day.' 'No, not that . . . it's Gee's birthday! Here's a card, get someone to send her masses of flowers, and they mustn't cost less than ten pounds.'

I was in San Francisco before the war when Gertie was playing 'Susan and God' at the Curran Theatre, and one evening we decided to make a tour of Chinatown. The Chief of Police offered to be our guide and off we went along the dark alleyways and up rickety staircases, pretending all the time we were risking the dangers that had not existed in years. A British warship happened to be on a courtesy visit to 'Frisco, and towards two in the morning we saw three able seamen swaying lightly in the middle of Grant Avenue. They affected both of us with nostalgia for home, and so we went up to make their acquaintance. By way of introduction, Gertie, in her delightful confident way, with the words going up and down the scale, said: 'I am Gertie Lawrence!' We waited in suspense for their reaction. 'I am Gertie Lawrence,' repeated Gertie, 'you know . . . the actress!' They looked at her a little unsteadily; then one of them mumbled: 'Well . . . if you are . . . sshow ush where we can get shome women!' Gertie pulled three ten dollar bills from her handbag and gave one to each bewildered, weaving seaman. Then she turned to the Chief of Police: 'I think these boys are looking for trouble . . . couldn't you arrange to get them back to the ship . . . gently?' And he did.

Gertie had a passionate love for England and during the war she was the driving force behind a transatlantic parcels service; then later, before and after the Normandy landings, she served in ENSA. One evening, after she had said goodbye at Drury Lane, ENSA headquarters, before returning to America, Jeannie and I were sitting with her in the Grill Bar of the Savoy. 'You know,' she said firmly, 'I have one ambition I am absolutely determined to fulfil.' Gertie was always able to wrap her ambitions in a rich canopy of sentiment, and this was no exception. Her voice changed, a hint of drama.

'That wonderful old theatre,' she went on, 'with all its traditions and glamour and triumphs . . . just think of the emotions it holds within its walls. I was thinking as I walked over here . . . I *must* play there!'

A few years later there was a memorable first night on Broadway at which Gertie triumphed as Anna in Rodgers and Hammerstein's 'The King and I'; and soon afterwards she wrote us a letter in which there was this line; 'Anna's staying two years on Broadway . . . and then THE first night at Drury Lane!' She was not to be there at that first night, for she died a few months after writing to us; but when the night came, Jeannie and I far away at Minack, thought of the gay audience making their way to their seats, the lights going down, the orchestra beginning to lilt the melodies she loved so much, and of the secret wish she never saw fulfilled.

We spent our last New Year's Eve in London with her and her husband Richard Aldrich, and I remember the gusto with which she led the Conga that threaded through the Savoy, boisterously enjoying herself; and I remember the toast she gave us that night after the trumpeters had blared their welcome to the New Year. 'Good luck to you escapists from the rat-race!'

Alas, the Princess of Wales violets in Gee's meadow did not prosper. Our wish to grow the particular variety had been dominated by the whim that we preferred it to any other, and that, of course, is no way to run a commercial flower farm; and the reason we liked it was because, unlike any other commercial variety, the blooms had an exquisite scent. We had been warned it was difficult to grow, that it bloomed sparsely, that the price obtained for the bunches did not recompense these disadvantages – and yet we had obstinately clung to the supreme confidence that in our case the results would be different. The runners bushed into plants and for a few brief weeks we thought our green fingers were going to succeed where others had failed – and then the plants collapsed. We hastily sought advice and the adviser diagnosed the microscopic red spider as the cause of the sickness, but here was a puzzle – red spiders thrive in dry conditions and yet the weather at the time was rain day after day, so wet that it was useless to spray the plants with the concoction which was recommended. Tommy too, was at a loss. 'I've always heard,' he said solemnly, 'that red spiders were bad sailors – yet here they be awash and living.'

Whatever the sickness the plants died and we have never

grown Princess of Wales again; but we do now grow a few scented violets of a variety called Ascania. We found it by chance growing wild in a hedgerow, a pale green leaf with a tiny bloom a soft purple in colour and with a scent so sweet and strong that a single small bunch perfumes a room. It is, I believe, the original Cornish violet which was discarded by growers long ago when the hybrid commercial varieties were introduced. It is still useless for sale on its own, but when we have time we add a bloom or two to the bunches we are sending to market and imagine the delight of those who receive them.

While Jeannie worked at her book, I picked the Governor Herrick in the big field. We have now at Minack certain jobs we call lady's jobs and others called gentleman's jobs; and of these, violet picking and bunching are clearly a lady's job. They are fiddling tasks requiring the deft fingers of a seamstress rather than the clumsy hand of a man; and whereas I plod along picking perhaps three dozen bunches an hour, Jeannie picks twice that number. A market bunch consists usually of twenty blooms and two leaves, so when we are picking we count the blooms until we have sixty odd, then collect the six leaves and slip a rubber band over the stalks of the lot; this in violet jargon is a field bunch, a bunch which is not too big to hold and a bunch that, at the end of the day's picking, enables you to know exactly the number of market bunches available.

The stalks are brittle and can easily be snapped off too short; and the blooms, if the plants are big ones, hide among the foliage so that unless you are painstakingly careful you can easily leave a bloom or two behind. You have to examine every bloom to see if it is marked – for there is nothing so irritating to a buncher as having to pick and choose between good and bad blooms; and the secret of speedy bunching is to be free of the responsibility of bloom choice. Normally the marked blooms you have to watch for are those whose petals have been nipped by tiny slugs and snails, insignificant holes but enough to spoil the whole bunch. But there are also the occasions when wind or frost or hail sweep through the plants leaving no bloom

109

undamaged; and then you have the nightmare task of picking not for market, but just to have the useless blooms off the plant.

Leaves are equally liable to damage and there is also a period during the season when they are often in short supply, and then we use ivy leaves in their place. This shortage, except when frost has done its harm, is due to a natural pause in the life of the plant, and it will occur once, or perhaps twice, during the October to April flowering season; the leaves go small like buttons, and yellow, and the crown of the plant is bared to the sky and for a week or two it seems as if the plant is dead; and then miraculously, little green shoots thrust upwards followed by the pin points of the buds, and soon the plants are in bloom again.

In the beginning I used to help Jeannie with the bunching but my laborious efforts, my groans as I fumbled with the stalks which swivelled this way and that in my fingers, became a handicap to her enthusiasm. She was so fast and I was so slow that I was like a runner who is lapped several times in a race; and her bunches were so much better than mine. I have seen professional violet bunchers who work at great speed show no regard as to the final look of the bunches; they gather the required number of blooms, add the leaves, slip on the rubber bands, and that, as far as they are concerned, is another bunch ready for market. Jeannie works as fast but she arranges every bloom to face the same way, so that when you hold up the bunch all the violets are looking at you, wide open like miniature pansies.

There is an art, too, in packing them in the flower boxes. First, however, after being bunched, their heads are dipped in water and the bunches are left overnight in jars filled to the brim with water; violets revel in wet and, as they drink through their petals, they will survive for days if they are dipped regularly. The bunches are packed tightly in the boxes but the number depends on whether they have short or long stalks, which in turn depends on whether it is cold or mild weather; when they are short Jeannie packs forty-two bunches, when long, thirty bunches; and she lays them on white tissue paper, the ends of which are folded over to cover the blooms before putting on the top. Then off the boxes go in the Land Rover to Penzance station and from there on the flower train to whichever market we have decided on; and in two or three days the price returns arrive through the post and we open the envelope in excitement. 'Sixpence!' I shout with delight. Or gloomily I murmur: 'Only threepence.'

It is a depressing experience, an experience which sets the mood for the day, when a box of flowers we have admired, which has caused Jeannie to shout from the flower house: 'You *must* come and see these before I put the top on . . . they're so beautiful!' — when such a box fetches a poor price. We feel cheated and angry, and we curse the salesman, and I scribble a note of complaint. Or we say stoutly: 'We won't send to *that* market again'. Just like the potatoes, just like anything else a market gardener grows . . . once a product is away from the packing shed it becomes a ticket in a lottery. Yet, as there is no alternative, as it is far too complicated a business to sell direct to retailers, one has to learn, like growing old, to accept the situation. We now accept it by sending our flowers regularly to the same salesman season after season. We send to Clifford Cowling at Leeds, the Dan Wuille Group, a firm in Birmingham and to Carlo Naef, the Italian born doyen of Covent Garden salesmen. They receive between them the whole range of our present day output – violets, anemones, daffodils, freesias, wallflowers, forget-me-nots, calendulas, polyanthus, Christmas flowering stocks; and if sometimes their price returns disappoint, enraging us, we have to admit to ourselves that they too are at the mercy of the same flighty mistress; the mysterious, intangible, elusive 'supply and demand'.

The first winter I cared not a rap for such economic factors because my imagination did not wish to grasp the prospect that they would ever beset me. I was doped by the sheer pleasure of being a peasant; by the plodding work that did not require mental activity; by day-end exhaustion that did not repay with worried, sleepless nights; by the pleasure of achievement after I had defeated the wind and the rain, and the baskets were filled with violets.

Physical effort is so much more gentle than that of the mind and, being new to it, I found it more rewarding. Mine was the pleasure of the mountaineer, the Channel swimmer or the marathon runner – enthusiasm allied with determination that brought victory which is sweet to the senses and provided tangible conquest in a personal battle. I was blessed at the time by the simple belief that flower growing was determined by obeying certain well defined rules, and success was automatic for him who did so; manure the ground, for instance, see there is enough lime, stick the plants in at the right time, and so on. I had, of course, to work hard and be ready to accept advice from experienced growers whenever I was in doubt, and pick their brains whenever I had the chance. I had, in fact, to behave like any intelligent man with initiative, and my reward would be flowers in abundance. I had not the slightest conception of the savage surprises ahead of me, nor of the bewildering contradictions that growing provides. Quite early on, during that first winter, however, my education was to begin.

The Princess of Wales had already disappeared and now the Governor Herrick started to look anaemic; and instead of lush green plants cascading violet blooms like those of my neighbours, they resembled row upon row of pale faced schoolboys in need of a holiday. The stalks were short, the length of my thumb; the blooms were like pin-points and the petals unwilling to open; and the leaves were grey-green and crinkly.

I am giving the wrong impression. They never at any time looked bursting with life, but a philosophy of wishful thinking convinced me they were certain to improve; and only the departure of autumn forced me to admit that something was radically wrong. My best week's picking had been twenty-four dozen bunches; and in view of the number of plants we had it should have been three times that number. 'What's wrong with the violets?' I said at last to Tommy. I was often to be amazed how Tommy, who was so intelligent on many subjects, was so ignorant on matters that directly concerned his profession; or perhaps his profession was to make use of his strength, leaving questions of skill to his bosses. 'They look sick,' was all the answer he could give me.

I had, I now realise, a child-like faith in the wisdom of those who lived close to the soil; and it never seemed possible to me that nature often defeated them. However, it never occurred to me, until experience proved it, that growers, like all experts, frequently offered advice that was diametrically opposite in its content. There was another occasion in another year when our violet runners failed from the beginning to take a grip with their roots; and I travelled the district, samples of dead runners in my hand, seeking an answer to the mystery.

Surely, I said to myself, these people who have been growing violets all their lives will be able to give me the answer; and yet each advanced a different theory none of which, as I learnt later, was the right one. I found out on my own that the damage had been inflicted by myself; in an effort to provide special food for each runner, I had dropped a handful of blood and bone mixture in each hole as I planted them, and this had burnt and killed the fibre roots.

As for the Governor Herrick, one man said the runners must have come from stock which had become exhausted, another that I could not have put any manure in the ground (I had put plenty of fish manure), and another that the wind had stunted the plants. Jeannie and I came to the conclusion that the latter explanation was the most likely one and we decided, after much discussion, to invest £30 in coconut netting and posts. The gesture, however, had a feeble result. It was too late. If a winter flowering plant of any kind has not become firmly established by early autumn, there is nothing you can do afterwards to bring it to life.

I have learnt now – and how costly the lessons have been – that you must anticipate trouble if you are to be a successful grower; you must be an optimist in the long term, a pessimist in the short, and you must be perpetually on guard against sudden attack by the elements, insects and diseases which are always in waiting to catch you off your guard.

Along the bank above the Governor Herrick we had

planted an assortment of daffodils which had come from Gordon Gibson, a famous grower in the Scilly Islands who was an old friend of Jeannie's family. It was not an ideal position for they faced the full blast of a Lizard wind, but we were short of space and the prize position in the wood had been given to 5 cwt. of King Alfred and 2 cwt. of Soleil d'Or. Nor for that matter were they fashionable daffodils; for daffodils like everything else can outlive popularity. We were, however, only too pleased to have them because we could not afford a stock of up-to-date bulbs, and any bulbs were better than none.

Each variety had arrived in the autumn with meticulous explanations from Gibson as to how they would look when the time came to bloom; Hospodar, for instance, coloured best when grown slowly in an open cool situation and would then have a deep orange red centre, in a warm season the colour would be poor; Campernelle, according to Gibson, was a dainty yellow scented jonquil, a lot of which could be packed in a box; Bernardino was white with a heavily frilled cup edged with apricot; Croesus was a mid-season variety with an orange red cup; Coverack Glory was a strong growing scented daffodil with a yellow trumpet. We were bewitched by these descriptions. We forgave the failure of the Governor Herrick in anticipation of this harvest of daffodils.

The first to bloom were the Soleil d'Or in the wood, and the first Sol in any year is a breath-taking moment that lifts the soul on a pinnacle, leaving it there high in the air to contemplate in exultation the wonder of the coming spring. This particular Sol appeared on a late January day, after a harassing morning during which, in our ignorance, we thought we had lost both the Soleil d'Or and all the King Alfred. During the night there had been a hard frost and when we went into the wood after breakfast we found the leaves and the stems quite flat – as if a roller had been driven over the meadow. It was a bitter moment. 'Well,' I said, 'that looks like the end of our daffodil crop.' But I was wrong and it took only a few hours for me to know it; for as the day brightened so did the leaves and stems

114

recover, and then suddenly we saw among the beds of the Soleil d'Or that solitary bloom; a button of yellow too beautiful to pick, its delicate scent touching the cold air like a feather.

Sols, like the early scented Scilly Whites, do not bloom uniformly, so unless you grow a large quantity you can never at one time send away in great numbers, their season protracts over weeks. King Alfreds, on the other hand, once a few blooms have heralded the way, rush in together crowding the meadow with buds. That first year they took us by surprise.

One day at the end of February we had picked a handful, the next I was lugging two baskets back to the cottage. 'Heavens,' I said to Jeannie, 'look at all these . . . and we haven't done a bunch in our lives!'

The remedy was to fetch our old friend Tom Bailey from Lamorna; here was a man who would not laugh at our enthusiasm nor our innocence. 'Tom,' I said, 'we've grown the flowers and now we haven't the slightest idea how to send them away!' I had found him bunching his own daffodils but he showed no irritation at the interruption. 'We'll soon put that right,' he grinned, 'come on, take me up to Minack and I'll show you.'

He was a good teacher because he had a high standard. There are many daffodil growers who seem to have no standards at all, no pride in a beautifully packed box; who bunch blooms however badly marked, jamming them into old cardboard boxes and wrapping them in newspapers if paper at all; farmers, for instance, who during the war and afterwards cashed in on the shortage of daffodils, growing them as if they were a field of turnips.

I once called on a farmer who showed me an outhouse filled with a white variety of daffodil standing in jars on the shelves with the petals stained the colour of autumn leaves. 'Caught the wind,' I said sympathetically, knowing that if they were mine they would all be thrown away. 'Damn nuisance,' he replied, adding blandly. 'I'm afraid it may affect the price.'

The reward for maintaining a high standard comes usually

when the markets are glutted with daffodils; and then buyers will ignore the rag and bobtail senders and stick to those whose standards are known. Our own aim is to send every box away from Minack as if it were going to an exhibition; and it is an aim that can only be achieved by having, at times, to dump large quantities of daffodils on the compost heap.

We ran into no trouble with those first King Alfreds, the weather was brisk but there was no strong winds to break the barrage of the wood and hurt them: and we picked when the buds had dipped at right angles to the stems and had begun to open, the yellow just showing. We brought them into the spare bedroom which Jeannie and her typewriter now vacated, and stood them in galvanised flower pails, perhaps for two days, until the bud formed its full beauty. Then we bunched them in twelves, finding the long firm stems easy to hold and arrange, boxed them in a bed of white paper a dozen bunches at a time, and then sent them off to Honor Bannerman, the head florist at the Savoy, who paid us a price far above anything we would have received in an ordinary market.

This, we said to each other, was a fine way of earning a living; and we had the further satisfaction of hearing of a man who so admired a bunch he bought at the stand in the Savoy's front hall, that he enquired where they came from, then ordered ten dozen to be sent to his friends. Pride, therefore, was mingled with the pleasure of profit; for we had found that in a fortnight's hectic activity we had earned enough to cover the capital outlay of the bulbs, and the bulbs were still there for many seasons to come. 'Just think,' I said to Jeannie with the gambler's aptitude to tot up prospective wins, 'we have taken £56 from 5 cwt. of bulbs . . . seven tons fill an acre, so if we could raise the capital to have that amount, we could earn over £1,500 a year!'

There was the beauty of the work as well. Tiredness, as known in other spheres, had no chance to conquer when the senses were being constantly refreshed by the tangible evidence of spring. Each morning we would enter the wood; then stop and marvel before we began to pick. Overnight

116

buds had dropped, opened and were peering their golden yellow over the green foliage, each with a destiny to provide delight. It was like a ballroom of child dancers, innocent and exquisite, brimmed with an ethereal happiness, laughing, loving, blind to passing time; and yet, almost unnoticed, day by day the flowers were leaving, then gathering speed, until suddenly there was only a floor of green, flecked here and there by a bloom that had stayed behind. The dance was over.

Along the bank in the field the Campernelle were flowering and beside them the Hospodar were thick with buds. Campernelle, Hospodar, Coverack Glory, Bernardino, Croesus . . . they would flower in that order, the poor relations of the King Alfred. We would not dare to despatch them to the Savoy, and we would take the luck of the markets; and yet we still had the advantage of being so far west that each variety would flower early, earlier than Lamorna, earlier than Coverack, earlier than Falmouth.

We were well satisfied with the shilling a bunch the Campernelle were fetching as thirty-six bunches were packed in a box; and then followed the Hospodar, first an odd bloom or two and suddenly a rush, stems clawing the air with nodding buds, a concourse of faces crowding the bank; and no sooner had these appeared than the Coverack Glory a little further down the field nearer the sea began drooping their yellow heads, demanding the attention we were giving to the others.

Up to then – it was the second week of March – the weather had been soft and warm, so gentle the wind one could not believe the gales of winter had ever existed, or could ever come again. Our only concern was to pick, bunch and send away. We had no time to anticipate trouble. We listened to the weather forecast but day after day it was so monotonously the same that there came an evening when we did not bother to turn on the wireless. The sky was clear, the sea still, and there was a pleasant security in the quietness, lulling us early to bed and quickly to sleep.

Suddenly I was awakened by a crash, and in the dimness I saw the curtains billowing before the open window like a sail torn from the mast. I fumbled for my torch and at the same time Jeannie cried out: 'My face cream! That was my new bottle of Dorothy Gray I left by the window!'

I had time neither to sympathise, laugh nor investigate the damage. It was the Lizard wind hissing through the trees, tearing into the daffodils that were scheduled to be picked in the morning.

'Hurry,' I said, 'we must get down to the field . . . ' and we pulled on our clothes and in a few minutes were fighting, heads down, against a gale that was to roar across Mount's Bay without pause for thirty-six hours. Our task was absurd, but ignorance at first made it appear feasible, the comfortable optimism at the beginning of a battle, the sheer stupidity of believing we could conquer the elements.

We had one torch which Jeannie held as I grapped at the waving stems, and unable to stand in the screaming wind we crawled on our hands and knees up and down the paths between the beds. For ten minutes we fought with the Hospodar and then, only a handful picked, I yelled to Jeannie: 'It's hopeless here . . . let's try the Coverack Glory!' Down we staggered to the lower part of the field and the beam of the torch shone on a sight which resembled a herd of terrified miniature animals tethered to the ground. Spray was now sticking to our faces and our hands, and a sense of doom was enveloping our hearts. We could not win. Nothing we could do would save our harvest.

9

FISHERMEN call the Lizard wind the starving wind, for the
fish hide from it on the bed of the sea and the boats return
empty to port. Landsmen solemnly call it the gizzard wind
as it bites into the body and leaves you tired when the day
is still young. It is a hateful wind, no good to anybody, drying the soil into powdery dust, blackening the grass like a
film of oil, punching the daffodils with the blows of a bully.
It is seldom a savage wind as it was on the night it destroyed
the Hospodar and Coverack Glory; if it were, if it spat its
venom then recoiled into quiet, you could cry over the
damage and forget. Instead it simmers its fury like a man
with a grudge, moaning its grievance on and on, day after
day, remorselessly wearying its victims into defeat.

The wasted stems of the Hospodar and the Coverack
Glory were piled high on the compost heap and now the
Bernardino and Croesus hastened to join them. Nothing
dramatic in their destruction, no sudden obliteration to
grieve over; the wind bit at each bud as it unfurled from the
calex, flapping the edge of a petal until it turned brown; or
it maliciously made the stems dance to its tune so that they
swayed together hither and thither, the buds rubbing and
chafing, bruising each other to an invisible end.

We watched and did nothing. As strangers to the wind
we bargained that any hour, any moment it might shift to
another quarter – hence we refused to buy coconut netting.
We considered moving that which surrounded the Governor Herrick, but perversely the plants were now hinting at
signs of growth; and, having waited so long, surely it would
be foolish to remove the protection that might at last ensure
us a reward? Thus we dithered, and hoped, and grew edgy.
Our income was blowing away before our eyes, and a little

of our confidence too; and when at last the wind moved round to the south it was too late. The Bernardine and the Croesus had enriched the compost heap while the violets, having demanded our loyalty, proved in due course their promised growth was a mirage.

The flowers were behind us and the potatoes ahead, and spring comes to Minack when people begin to ask: 'Are the taties covering the rows?' Lobstermen were dropping their pots and I had excitedly told Jeannie I had seen the first swallow skimming the coast line from its landfall near Land's End. The green woodpeckers were laughing again in the wood at hilarious jokes of their own and I would lie abed in the morning listening to the tap-tap-tap of one carving a hole in an elm. Sea pinks plumed from fat green cushions. A bat fluttered briefly as dusk fell. Robins pounced on worms and hurried off to an early brood. Foxes were bold, appearing casually in daylight in places where winter saw only a shadow. Wrens flighted with feathers bigger than themselves. A male mistlethrush wooed his lady by absurdly building a nest ten yards from our door. Monty looked gorgeous, his fur a glistening titian, as he stalked through the lush green grass. Bluebells abounded. Primrose lit the banks with their soft yellow, beckoning you to bury your face in their fragrance. There were the regular signs repeated year after year, bringing centuries together and denying the passage of time, shining security in a brittle present, taunting the desperation of beehive cities. If a man could not be at peace among them his shadow must be the enemy.

John again was the first to draw his potatoes and as the cart lumbered up from his cliff, I saw the glint in Tommy's eye. 'Better try ours tomorrow,' he grunted. The same old envy ricocheting down the coast – Tregiffian, Boscawen, St Loy, Penberth; all the way shovels were poised, eyes watching neighbours, silver tongued salesmen angling for custom, neat little meadows falling down the cliffs grinning at the sea and green with hope.

'Started drawing yet?' . . . 'Samples any good?' . . . 'Joe's digging two hundredweight a lace' . . . 'Where are you sending?' . . . 'Manchester is strong, Birmingham is weak'

122

: . . 'A shower won't do any harm' . . . 'Farmers will be early this year.'

John's meadows were round a shoulder of the cliff, facing due south and gaining an hour of sun over our meadows which fell into shadow in the late afternoon. That hour's sun meant a week in earliness, and nothing Tommy could do would alter the fact. Thus the ceremony of trying out stems was doomed to failure.

'We'll wait a few days,' I said to Tommy, 'no use murdering them.'

I was not, however, as calm as I appeared, for I too was gripped again with potato fever. It was a deliciously buoyant sensation. Here we were on the edge of retrieving our misfortunes of the flower season. The precious prospect of hitting the jackpot lay ahead, and if I did not wish to appear anxious to Tommy, it certainly did not matter how I appeared to Jeannie. 'Come on,' I said after Tommy had gone home, 'let's go and explore on our own.' It was a gesture of curiosity, not of expectation and we completed the formality without disappointment. 'Another week,' I said, 'at least another week.' And in that week Jeannie, Monty and I gained a companion who, when I started to dig, followed me up and down the row wagging his tail. His name was Gold Bounty.

Gold Bounty was a friendly black greyhound, and his arrival at Minack occurred in this way. A few years before, the White City had offered Jeannie a greyhound to run in her name, and invited us down to the kennels at Barnes to meet it. We were introduced to Gold Bounty who greeted us with such affection, so trustingly muzzled his face in Jeannie's hand, that she wanted to take him back to Mortlake immediately. We were limited, however, to occasional visits to the kennels, but there came a time when he knew us so well that he began to whimper and yelp in excitement as soon as he heard our voices in the corridor.

One day the manager said to us laughingly: 'Well, I can see that Bounty's going to have a good home when he retires.' We, too, laughed in reply. It was a long time off before such a thing would happen. Horizons away, and in the meantime he had races to win. This public side of his life began in sensational fashion; sensational at any rate, and delightful, for Jeannie and myself. When Gold Bounty made his début, we were having dinner in the glass-fronted terrace of the stadium with Don Iddon, the outspoken columnist of the *Daily Mail*, and A. P. Herbert, whose devotion to greyhound racing and football pools has brought him much frustration; and Jeannie was relaxing in the glow of being an owner whose dog was about to race, a situation which has its hazards, as she was later to find out.

For instance, the most unlikely people would sidle up to her: 'See Bounty's running tonight. What's his chances?' The craving for inside knowledge nurtured the delusion that the owner possessed that knowledge. Thus if Jeannie appeared in a mood of optimism, that mood would be responsible for a flow of whispers: 'Bounty's going to win tonight.' If she shrugged her shoulders and said she did not know, the converse was concluded. Unfortunately, she never possessed any secret information, and thus she deserved neither the smiles nor the black looks which followed her imaginary tips.

Indeed as Gold Bounty pursued his career he became a source of embarrassment to ourselves, for loyalty demanded we should back him but circumstances often made us forget; and the times we forgot were those when it seemed he most often won. But there was one awful occasion when he and another greyhound which had been presented to Jeannie called Corporal Mackay, both won on the same night, at combined odds of one hundred and fifty to one. We had not a penny on either. The trainer had told us before racing began that neither had the ghost of a chance.

Gold Bounty's first appearance resulted in a win by a short head after a photo finish. He came up round the last bend from fourth place in the red jacket of Trap Number One, and pipped the favourites on the post. We were hysterical. Alan Herbert shouted like a busker, Don Iddon filled our glasses with champagne, Jeannie stood on a chair yelling: 'Bounty! Bounty! Well done Bounty!' and I shook the hands of everyone at the next table, all of whom were strangers. The custom is for the greyhounds filling the first three places to be walked round the arena after each race; and Jeannie and I ran down to the rails to see Gold Bounty as he passed. He was a beautiful looking greyhound, not very big, and he walked as if on springs. 'Well done, Bounty!' we called. For a moment he looked in our direction, then barked. 'Oh what a good dog am I,' he seemed to be saying. He raced at the White City for four years; always genuine and intelligent, he was loved by the crowd, and many a night I have heard the arena filled with the roar: 'Bounty! Bounty! Come on Bounty!'

Then came the letter from the manager of one of the kennels saying it was time for Bounty to retire. Would we have him? Otherwise he would have to be put to sleep since he was not of high enough class to be of use at stud. Of course we agreed immediately to do so. At the same time we realised we were heading for trouble. Track greyhounds, being trained all their lives to chase the electric hare, had also the habit of chasing any other small animal on four legs. How could we keep Bounty and Monty apart?

We shut our minds to this problem in the excitement of his impending arrival, and when one late afternoon he was led from the guard's van of the Cornish Riviera we were waiting on the Penzance platform to give him a hero's welcome. He greeted us as old friends, barking excitedly and leaping up on his hindlegs. He was home. We had not let him down. He was going to have a wonderful time!

But as soon as we returned to the cottage we were faced with the reality of the problem with which we had landed ourselves. Monty, whom we had left shut up indoors, met us with an enraged glare from the window; Bounty saw him and started to bark furiously.

'Look,' I said to Jeannie, 'I'll take Bounty for a walk while you try and make peace with Monty.'

Monty never took any notice of a dog if it passed by him when he was on his own; but if we were about his back would arch, his fur rise, and then wham! . . . he would attack. In his own mind I suppose he was protecting us, but his ferocious behaviour was certainly startling to his victims.

Jeannie's cousin once called unexpectedly and arrived at the door holding a terrier in her arms. In an instant Monty was at it, and five minutes later the wretched girl herself was having first-aid in the bathroom. The same kind of episode happened time and time again, and the odd thing was this . . . whenever we rushed out to warn any visitor with a dog, we were always greeted with the same lofty remark: 'Our dog never goes for cats . . . you don't have to worry.'

We, therefore, knew from the beginning that Bounty would never be able to stay with us, although in the moment of welcome we had conveniently forgotten the fact. Our idea was to keep him at Minack for a few days and then to find him a permanent home; sensible but unwise, because every minute he spent with us our hearts became more emotionally involved. He was my shadow. He trotted trustingly at my heels when I took him for long walks, and when I started to shovel out the potatoes he followed me up the meadow, foot by foot, as if he thought his presence was essential. I would return to the cottage with him gambolling beside me, there to find poor old Monty sitting as usual in the window with fire in his eyes.

The nights were chaotic. Our intention had been for Bounty to use the potato hut as a kennel while Monty continued his custom of sleeping on the bed. But Bounty tore at the door and the walls and howled like a hyena until we were driven to silencing him by despatching Monty into the sitting-room, and bringing Bounty into the bedroom. A sliding door divided the enemies and rather than risk one of them slipping through when we opened it, we hopped in and out of the windows. Such a strain could hardly last and its end was sudden.

Jeannie had gone up to the farm to fetch the milk and had taken Bounty with her, and I had stayed behind to weed the garden. Suddenly I saw her running towards me up the lane. She was alone. 'It's happened!' she cried out as she reached me. 'What's happened?' I said, and saw her anguish.

'Bounty's killed a cat and he let out that awful howl as they do when they catch the hare!'

It's a blood curdling sound, a siren of the jungle. 'He must go! He must go!' It was an old cat, a dying one at that, and the farmer who owned it eased our minds by saying he would have had to kill it in any case. But we could not keep Bounty any longer. The honeymoon of his retirement was over.

That afternoon we put him in the back of the Land Rover and set off to find him a home. He thought it great fun. He put his paws on the back of my seat and pushed a wet nose in my neck; and he barked out of the sheer joy of barking. As for ourselves, we were remembering the roars of the White City crowds: 'Bounty! Bounty! Come on Bounty!' – and comparing this memory with the incongruous present; and as happens when one deceives an animal we felt humiliated.

Yet we knew we could find him a good home in St Buryan parish, for it has an ancient tradition of coursing and of breeding greyhound champions of the show ring. And we did. Trethewey looked at Gold Bounty with a grin on his face, and scratched his head in wonderment that such a beautiful dog was being given to him. He had three other greyhounds on his farm, and five minutes was enough to see that he was gentle with them; so we said good-bye to old Bounty feeling assured that he had many years of happiness before him. And it seemed we were right when, a few weeks later, we called and found Bounty curled up in the best armchair by the fire.

The next time I saw Trethewey was three months later when he knocked at the door of the cottage. 'Hello, Mr Trethewey,' I said cheerfully, 'how's Bounty?' He looked at me quietly for a moment. 'He's dead,' he said, 'he died last night of a heart attack.'

*   *   *

We ached our way once again through the potato harvest, and when it was all over and we had counted our takings, we were pleased by the immediate present, but disturbed by the future. We had had a good crop and fair prices, but viewed with dispassion we had to admit the outgoings were proving greater than income. The bliss of the first excursion was being tempered by the knowledge that we had embroiled ourselves in a business that had a considerable appetite. The element of wage paying demanded capital expenditure in order to provide it; thus experience at Minack was beginning to teach us the truth of Parkinson's Law.

If, for instance, you have an acre of land, you may be able to crop it yourself but the work is so exacting and returns so limited that you are certain to decide that you must increase your turnover by cropping more land; and this means you must have labour to help you. More land means more fertilisers, seeds, equipment and general overhead expenses all of which, added to the wage you now have to pay, cancel out the value of the increased turnover. An itch thereupon gets in your mind which worries you into believing that yet more capital expenditure is the answer. If you buy a motor hoe and so lessen the use of the hand hoe, if you buy a motor scythe and dispense with the old-fashioned hand one, if you buy a rotovator and give up digging the ground, if you buy . . . all these purchases, you say, will increase efficiency, spare labour for extra work, and thus bring nearer the elusive margin of profit.

You find the magic result does not materialise, yet the nagging thought develops that you have not been bold enough. What about a greenhouse? And if one greenhouse does not earn what you expect, what about two? Perhaps on the other hand you ought to increase your stock of bulbs, or have a new packing shed, or would it be better to invest in cloches? The ideas for expenditure roll out of your mind as if on a conveyor belt, and you lie awake at night and pace your room in the morning, tussling as to which idea to put into practice.

Funds meanwhile are falling low and instalment commitments increasing. A compelling force drives you to give up your intention of having a new suit in favour of the fertilisers the advisory officer urges you to spread over the bulb ground. Fertilisers, you argue, will increase next year's turnover while a new suit will rest most of the time in the cupboard. You realise by now that you are the victim of your own enthusiasm. So much money has been spent, so much energy expended, that retreat means disaster, and you are drawn by a magnet into a future which is grey with doubt. If the daffodils bloom in profusion, if they do not coincide with a glut, if the violets or anemones are not killed by frost, if it is not a bumper year for everyone else's tomatoes, if the potato plants are not blackened by gales, if their harvest does not have to compete with shiploads of foreign imports . . . then you may expect the year's endeavour to earn you a living.

Market garden efficiency cannot be classified in the same way as a factory. For one thing there is no roof to protect you from the weather; for another you cannot put your goods in a stockroom until there is a demand for their sale because your goods begin to die after they are gathered; and you cannot possibly draw up an accurate budget as you have little idea of what your output may be, and not the faintest notion what price your goods will fetch. Placid looking market gardeners, therefore, are inveterate gamblers and their life is not, as it appears, a plodding one. It dwells in high excitement, and the charm of it is that the grey doubts of the future are invariably quelled by titillating prospects of a new season.

Meanwhile we devised means to live cheaply, and in such efforts the countryman has the advantage over the townsman. Appearances, unless you leave the compound, do not matter and thus old clothes which, in a city, would have been pushed into retirement, continue in rough service for year after year. Rents are a fraction in comparison and nagging bills such as those for warming the house in winter can be tempered by taking a walk and collecting your own logs. You can have your own fresh eggs and by growing vegetables you can spend the townsman's contribution to the greengrocer on something else.

Jeannie and I now began to wonder whether we could catch our own fish in some manner which would not necessitate my dangling a rod for hour after hour when I should be doing something else. I considered the merits of the kite which is used by off-shore lighthouse keepers. This kite with baited hook attached is set off before the wind until it is far

129

enough away to be pulled down into the sea, and then is reeled into the rocks beneath the lighthouse. Such a kite is independent of which way the wind is blowing but obviously, if I were to use a kite, I would only be able to launch it when the wind was blowing off the land.

I then had the idea of a toy clockwork motor-boat sailing out to sea from our rocks attached to a line which I would hold, and towing a short second line with a swivel hook attached. This swivel hook would provide the same effect as one being pulled by a fishing boat, luring perhaps mackerel which are rarely caught within casting distance of the rocks – pollock being the normal catch. I found, however, that clockwork did not have the power to face the sea, and any other model was far too expensive. I thereupon settled for a lobster pot.

But a lobster pot still did not provide the answer. We had an ideal spot to drop it, a rock which jutted out into the small bay then fell sheer to the water so that even at low tide it was thirty feet deep. Our method of operation was to weight the pot with stones, bait it with gurnet which we collected from Newlyn fish market, and throw it with a splash into the sea, watching it gurgle its way to the depths. The connecting rope was fastened to a ring we had cemented in a hole in the rocks – one of several holes each a few inches wide which obviously had been man-made for some mysterious reason in the distant past.

Then we left the pot for twenty-four hours in hopeful expectation that lobsters and crabs would crawl to their doom. We had good reason for hopefulness because the lobstermen themselves dropped their pots out in the cove within a stone's throw of our rocks; and so what was likely to go into their pots had only to travel a few yards to go into our particular one. They did not bother to do so. Our total catch in eight weeks consisted of several useless spider crabs, one lobster, and a three-foot conger eel whose fang-like teeth gave me the fright of my life as I fought for half an hour to extract it from the pot. I was proud of this conger eel and I carried it up the cliff to the cottage as if I were Monty boasting the catch of a mouse. 'Look!' I said to Jeannie, 'look what I've caught!' The dead eyes leered at her, the grey elongated body was slimy in my hands. Quickly I realised my pride was misplaced. 'It's horrible,' she said, 'take it away out of my sight!'

Then one evening in the Mousehole pub we met a fisherman called Ned who described a trammel net to us; and he made it sound so alluring that we concluded we would be able to catch enough fish to supply not only ourselves but our neighbours as well. The technicalities were these.

The trammel net was fifty yards long, six feet deep and had a two-inch mesh. Weights were fastened at intervals along one length of the net and corks along the other, specially balanced so that the net floated six feet deep from the surface of the sea. Normally the net was used by either end being attached to two boats, so that they swept the fishing ground like a minesweeper; but Ned's proposal was that we should adjust this principle to our particular conditions which demanded, of course, that we should 'shoot' the net from the rocks and use a buoy anchored in the cove with a pulley attached. The net had long ropes at either end and one of these was threaded through the pulley, then brought back to the rocks; so that when we 'shot' the net we would haul one rope to send it out to sea, and haul the other when we brought it ashore, both ropes of course being at other times securely tied to the rings we had cemented in the holes in the rocks.

One morning, therefore, when the sea in the cove appeared as quiet and innocent as a cow musing in a meadow, Ned nosed in his boat and dropped overboard a 56 lb. weight with the buoy attached about sixty yards out from where Jeannie and I were standing on the rocks. He had with him the net and the ropes, one of which he threaded through the pulley; then, feeding the net over the side of the boat into the sea, he edged his way towards us until he was near enough to throw the rope-ends which we promptly fastened to the rings. Thus the trap was set and we could see the shadow of the net stretching half-way across the cove; all we had to do was to go away and think of the fish swimming into it.

For a couple of weeks they obliged to such an extent that we had fish for breakfast, lunch and dinner while Monty stuffed himself with plateful after plateful. The snag was, however, that it was always the same fish – pollock – and we grew sick of the sight of it. True we also caught the bony, many coloured, uneatable rass, but these were thrown back into the sea; there was never a sign of the fish of the fishmonger's slab, the mullet, bass and mackerel. The hope they would come remained. Every day at low tide we went down to the rocks and pulled in the net, picked out the fish, then 'shot' the net once again. The weather was fine and the task was simple except for one aspect; and this was to prove our undoing. There was no clear run between the buoy and where I stood pulling in the net. I had to stand in such a position that the net had to be dragged on a jagged channel of rocks close to the water line, and where in fact we picked out the fish. Inevitably I stood the risk of tearing the net but, heavy and cumbersome as it was to control, there was little danger of doing this while the weather was calm; and if it were rough Ned had already warned us to untie it from the ropes and hoist it far out of danger on to the upper part of the rocks – for if the net was out in the cove when a gale blew up, it would certainly be lost.

The first gale caught us prepared, or so we thought. We heard the warning on the six o'clock shipping forecast, and raced down the cliff, pulled in the net and carried it high and dry above the rocks. As I have said, the net was heavy and when just out of the water, felt like a ten ton weight; so it took time to get it to safety, and the effort brought a sense of satisfaction.

Around midnight I was wakened by such a convulsion of wind roaring round the cottage that I began to worry whether we had taken the net high enough up the rocks. The old nagging worry of the wind which chased us always at Minack; lying cosily in bed with a sound outside like tube trains rushing; as if the cottage had angered a madman who was jabbing at it with a madman's venom. Hate in the wind. Merciless with a bully's power. Wedging a stick of conscience as I lie in bed and listen and fear. Was I careful enough? or did I only pay court to care? Was I lazy because the day was still, my imagination dull? The seasons lie behind me and the wreckage of the wind cuts into my memory like a general remembering the dying in a lost battle.

At one a.m. Jeannie and I got up and dressed and lit a hurricane lamp, and with heads down against the wind, the light spangling the dancing grasses at our feet, we struggled down the cliff. The seas were enormous. Spray wetted our faces like a sponge and the white crests of the waves rib-boned the rocks; and it did not take an instant for us to realise that the net had been dragged from its safety.

'It's my fault,' I shouted, 'I should have taken it further up!' So easy to self-blame when the exception had occurred; such admission softens, too, the disappointment. And yet that night the waves were lunging at rocks, high above the water line we had never seen wet before; where wayward seeds had fertilised, like meadow sweet and sea pinks and wild alyssum, in crevises of wind-blown soil. We staggered forward oblivious of the danger, enraged that care in our fashion had been rewarded by the cheat of the sea. Then, as we stood amid the shower of the waves with the lamp swing-ing in my hand, I suddenly saw the net stretched like a straddled whale along the rocks; for one instant in black relief in the lamp-light, the next lost in the mouth-wash of the sea.

I gave Jeannie the lamp and she held it above her head, the light shining on her salt-wet face, feebly acting as sentinel, eyeing the gush of water as it recoiled from the rocks, reflecting the quiet pause, flickering a warning as a white mass gathered momentum then crashed in a thousand fragments splintering the night with spray. At each pause I dashed forward and tugged at the net. I loosened it first from one crevice, then another, and above the thunderous noise Jeannie would shout: 'Quick! Come back! Another one coming!' I struggled as if with an octopus, bit by bit, further and further from the water line until the waves no longer grasped with hands but clawed with fingers instead, becoming weaker, strength in spasms, until impotent and defeated they could only stretch at the net as if to caress.

The next morning we looked at the damage, and it was not as bad as we had expected. We laboured up the cliff and took the net to the fisherman's store in Newlyn where we had bought it. It remained there for three weeks during which time an old salt patiently repaired it. By now the net had cost us over £20, and the fish it had so far produced had been highly expensive; but the summer was still young and the lesson to take greater care well learnt. We listened to the forecasts and whenever there was a suggestion of wind we pulled in the net and piled it high up on the rocks.' Such methodical caution was admirable provided the forecasts were correct, but one Sunday evening when the net was stretched across the cove, the sea as still as a saucer of milk, the sky clear, the forecast promised the same quiet weather would continue for the next twenty-four hours – yet within twelve the sea was a cauldron.

As dawn broke behind the hills on the other side of Mount's Bay, I was straining with all my might to bring in the net, but just as part of it reached the channel of rocks where it lay when we picked out the fish, the pulley jammed on the buoy that was bobbing like a cork out in the cove. I was in any case in danger and Jeannie was yelling to me to retreat. I watched for a moment the net swirling in the waters and wrapping itself round the jagged points of the rocks like a black serpent. This was good-bye to our fish. No chance would arise now to carry the net like a wounded animal to Newlyn. The sea had exacted its revenge.

10

ONE summer the violets were in the meadow below the cottage which had been a bog when we first arrived, and where Tommy and I had sunk yards of earthenware drain pipes. I was weeding the plants one afternoon when Jeannie, who had gone for a walk over the cliffs, returned highly excited. The delight of her character was the way in which her zest relished our adventure in a manner so natural, so persuasive in its truth, that never at any time did she fail to enthuse even when I, crowding my mind with materialistic fears, blocked her enthusiasm with doubts.

I doubted, for instance, on this occasion when she bubbled the news that the farmer whose land bordered John's to the west, five minutes' walk from Minack, was prepared to rent us two acres. These particular acres together with a cascade of small meadows which fell to the sea below them and which the farmer was to retain for himself, had a reputation in the district of being a potato gold mine. It was a reputation which stemmed from the war, when new potatoes fetched ten shillings a pound and daffodils of the most common variety five shillings a bunch. It was early land facing south with the Wolf Rock a finger in the distance, so early that the farmer concerned had never failed to keep his record of sending the first mainland potatoes to market. Thus Pentewan, as the land was called, seemed to provide the chance we were seeking. We were cramped at Minack, but now we could launch out as big growers.

'I wonder why he's giving it up?' I said to Jeannie. My hesitancy was a poor reward for her enthusiasm and she told me so bluntly, nor was my caution to be relied upon. It was a mood which might well be concerned with my dissatisfaction over the growth of the plants I was hoeing, a trivial moment of gloom unfitted to greet a challenge. It certainly was unfair to Jeannie.

'He says there'll be room for four tons of potatoes,' she went on as if she were trying to put a match to my woodiness, 'so that with four tons over here we'll have eight tons of seed next year and at three and a half to one that means twenty-eight tons of potatoes. We could take at least a thousand pounds, and with luck much more!'

If her reasoning sounded optimistic, it also made sense. We had cropped eleven tons of potatoes from three tons of seed during the past season and had averaged £45 a ton; thus Pentewan together with the land we were continuing to reclaim at Minack would put us firmly in sight of establishing ourselves. We would have elbow room, space for more bulbs, be able to grow a greater variety of crops and each on a substantial scale if we so wished. It would counter the disadvantage of Minack where, in view of the endless reclaiming that had to be done, we resembled two people living in a house that was in the process of being built. At Pentewan the meadows awaited us, old hands which knew what was expected of them, a century of sun-drenched labour within their boundaries. I had become as excited as Jeannie.

Meanwhile Jeannie's *Meet Me At The Savoy* for which Danny Kaye had written the foreword had sold as a serial to *John Bull*, and we had invested the proceeds in making the cottage our own particular palace. We installed a petrol-driven pump at the top of the well and became reacquainted with the comfort of a bath and indoor lavatory, having added a wood-built annexe at the far end of the one-time chicken house. This development – hot water came from a calor gas heater – gave us as much pleasure as that of a millionaire sailing a maiden voyage in his yacht. We revelled in our independence of the weather, and the gush of a tap gave us the same sharp wonderment as that of natives being introduced to the plumbing civilisation for the first time. We still could not afford a sink with running water from a day and night burning stove, nor a hole through the end wall of the cottage with a connecting lobby to the spare room and bathroom; and it was two years before we could do so. Thus, in order to reach the bathroom, we had to go through the front door, a task which was inconvenient but not disastrous; and as far as the washing up was concerned we had to continue to use a basin, then empty the contents over a neighbouring hedge.

I sometimes wonder whether the ghosts of the cottage cast a spell over us, enabling us to accept this abuse of twentieth-century comfort in the way we did. Inconvenience had pervaded the cottage for over five hundred years, so was it inevitable that we should act as if it were natural? The twentieth century decorates life like a Christmas cake, but it still cannot do anything about the basic ingredients; and there seemed to be a starkness in our companionship which enabled us to find a fulfilment without the aid of man-made devices; as if the canvas of each day was so vast that mirror-smooth techniques of living, coma entertainment like television, would only make it unmanageable. We are still without electricity and we remain thankful we have no telephone; yet it would be a pose to pretend that self denial did not seek its compensations.

We have revelled in occasional brisk returns to the life we used to know, being flattered because we were new faces in an old circle or rejoicing in the stimulation of reunions. It was fun being at the first night of A. P. Herbert's musical play 'The Water Gipsies' which he wrote at Minack, to stay at the Dorchester because Richard Aldrich wanted us to be present when his book *Gertrude Lawrence as Mrs A* was launched. All this was the sugar that titivates a day but does not provide its bread; and the basic fact remained that we could not build Minack by playing as if it were an accessory to our life instead of its foundation.

These sorties to an existence which used to be our daily round confirmed the wisdom of our escape, but, at the time, we were doped by the paraphernalia of sophistication. We delighted in the silliness, the laughter in cocktail bars, relaxing late in the afternoon over lunch, parties at night. No one could have called us peasants. But when we returned to Minack we looked back on those gilded shadows and were thankful they had passed over us so briefly. We felt pity instead of envy for our contemporaries whose company had regained for us so much pleasure. Success in this age breeds only a rackety happiness, providing little time for its own enjoyment. The bite of competition is too sharp for leisure, so success is either pimped by others to further their own ends or creates its own demoralisation and betrays the truth from which it sprang. There is no freedom in twentieth-century achievement for the individual is controlled not by his own deep thinking processes but by the plankton of shibboleths which are currently in fleeting fashion; and by his own desperate need to maintain financial survival in the glittering world he has found himself. Jeannie and I have also to fight for survival, but it is an easy battle compared to that in a city. At least the countryman still possesses the luxury of being able to live at the same leisurely pace of another age.

*　　*　　*

We took over Pentewan meadows and briskly decided to cultivate them by modern methods. They were, for the most part, large sloping meadows which from time immemorial had been shovel-turned in the autumn, shovel-planted with potatoes in early spring, shovel-cropped in the summer. They had never seen a machine, and even the laborious task of hacking the ground into suitable condition before planting had always been done by hand. Obviously my new landlord had found an extra man would be needed on the farm if the meadows were to be worked, and unless the wage was that of a coolie profits would be small; and in any case he could not be bothered with the trouble that labour in such circumstances often involves.

I, on the other hand, untrammelled by tradition, was convinced that the answer to the problem was mechanisation; and that once I had gathered around me the correct assortment of machines I would forge ahead with the same relentless success as a gang on a motorway. I was not thinking in terms of the normal sized tractors but of the hand-controlled variety, one of which I had already tried out at Minack; and

I thought that if I had a motor-hoe and a motor-driven hedge cutter, tedious time absorbing tasks would be cut to the minimum.

I bought the Minack tractor second-hand, a monstrous looking thing with a plough, and an engine that kicked like a mule every time I started it. Tommy, who could handle any horse, had nothing in common with this example of progress, and he behaved to it always as if he were a fox sniffing danger; and when one day I suddenly saw Tommy careering down the big field towards the cliff, hanging on to the handlebars with the tractor quite out of his control, I decided it was time to get rid of it.

It was exchanged for a second-hand rotovator and this was the machine with which we first went into the attack on the Pentewan meadows. It was a dual purpose machine for if I exchanged the normal small wheels for large ones, removed the rotovator from the engine and substituted a specially designed shaft I could use it with a plough; and a plough can sometimes do work for which a rotovator is useless. For instance some experts will say that a rotovator used often on the same ground will pommel it into uselessness; and that ground should be spared the rotovator and ploughed instead at least once every two years. This probably applies where blades are used but in this instance I had claw-like tines fitted to the machine which churned the soil as if they were forks being used at maniacal speed. The theory was right but the execution wrong, because every time a tine hit a rock hidden beneath the soil it would snap; and as there were many such rocks this method became ridiculously expensive.

I soon found, too, that the machine did not like me; for time and again when I set out to rotovate, the engine obstinately refused to start. Usually, of course, on such occasions the fault can be quickly corrected by a mechanic, and the mechanic if you possess the most elementary knowledge should be yourself. Check plug, clean carburettor, make sure the ignition is all right . . . I used to perform these tasks, secure no result, then storm back to Jeannie. 'The bloody thing won't work,' I would shout, 'and I'll have to get them to come and see it.'

'Them' were the Helston people from whom I had bought it, and in due course a kindly mechanic would arrive, tinker an hour or two with the engine, gain no response, then remark: 'I've never known an engine like this before.' My years at Pentewan – and other rotovators behaved in the same way as this first one – are filled with memories of mechanics in various meadows where the rotovator of the moment had broken down, unscrewing things, screwing things up, with me beside them hopefully staring, waiting for them to arrive, or thanking them for coming. 'I can't help thinking,' said one, grimly trying to be cheerful, 'if the firm wouldn't be wise to pitch a tent here.'

Yet this first rotovator had the advantage of being the spearhead of our hopes; and the tantrums were forgiven because we were, in our own minds, revolutionising the cultivation of cliff meadows. Others might think their commercial value wsa dying out but we were proving that a new outlook, a dashing grasp of experts' advice, would lead them to prosperity. Our landlord had a man called Joe who looked after the cascade of meadows below our own, vineyards of meadows where no machine of any kind could reach, falling to the sea amid hedges of escallonia, apple trees, and banks thick in winter with the fragrance of wild violets; and Joe would leave a meadow which he had been laboriously turning with a shovel, and come to watch me at work; to stare at my method of rotovating or perhaps just to help me with advice on how to get the engine started.

Joe belonged to the cliffs in the same way that a cliff fox or a cliff badger belongs; and he disapproved of change in the same way that anyone disapproves of action that changes something directly concerning his own heart. He distrusted the rotovator. He would stand at the bottom of the meadow where I was working, an old felt hat on his head, a pipe in his mouth, eyes that were set wide apart, young middle age, looking at me bringing the rotovator down the hill then reversing upwards, my foot on the metal cover to keep it from lurching the handlebars high from my grasp. He would watch and say nothing, chewing the stem of his pipe; and then weeks later I would be in some pub, and I would be told: 'I hear that that there rotovator brings all the soil down bottom of meadow.' I do not agree that this view was right; but it made me aware that Joe as he meandered from his own particular world so near the sea, was watching and judging me as I bent the ways of the clinical present to better the integrity of the past; and so I, too, watched and listened.

Joe used to bicycle to the cliffs from his home with Bish his bull terrier trotting at the wheel; and when Bish grew old Joe carried him on the handlebars. Like all his breed Bish was a fierce protector of his owner and of his owner's belongings and as we shared the same hut there were often occasions when Bish would not allow us to enter. The hut was known as the Pink Hut because it was built of corrugated-iron once painted a red which had faded to pink over the years; and as its main function was for the 'shooting' of potatoes it was so designed inside that layer upon layer of boards could be fixed, each layer rising above another which had received its quota of potato seed. Joe had one half of the hut with its boards, we had the other; and there were times when we wanted to use our half when only Bish was resident in the other. Then Bish, so friendly when nothing of his owner's was threatened, would bare his teeth, snarl, bellow, and frighten us into cupping hands to mouth and shouting downwards towards the sea: 'Joe! Joe! Come up will you? Bish won't let us in!' There would be an answering cry like the hoot of an owl, and in a few minutes Joe would slowly arrive, and Bish would wag his tail and grin at us and apologise.

Joe accepted wild life, not as some countrymen do with the object to kill, but as a means of sharing enjoyment. He hated trapping and when on one occasion he was instructed to do so, he found the next morning in one of the traps a badger. A badger is notoriously, and for obvious reasons, a deadly dangerous animal to release from a trap; and a trapper, if for no other reason except his personal safety, will make certain he had killed it before there is any question of touching it. Not so Joe. He was grievously upset when

143

he found the badger struggling to escape as he walked along the field towards it; and he decided the only thing he could do was momentarily to stun it, then quickly release the foot from the trap. He picked up a stick and hit it, and the badger lay still. Ten minutes later it was still lying there, breathing but without any other signs of life; and so Joe picked it up in his arms, a heavy full grown badger, and carried it gently to the Pink Hut.

I came to the hut later in the morning when Joe was having his tea break, and found the badger lying on a bed of sacks, with another sack so folded that it acted as a pillow. Bish was quiet in another corner. Joe puffing his pipe. 'I hit it too hard,' he said to me sadly after he had told me what had happened, 'that's what I did. I hit it too hard.'

Jeannie and I were, at the time, 'shooting' potatoes and this tedious task kept us for hour upon hour in the hut. This gave us the advantage of keeping an eye on the patient as it lay there. It was early in the afternoon over twenty-four hours later that it stirred, an eye opened, and it whimpered. A badger is beautiful to look at in its true setting, a wild path of its own treading, the moon lighting the white streaks of its head, dark shadows its armour; but lying there in the hut, impotent without our help, a heavy immovable body, its appeal was not in its mobility but the common denominator of suffering. I went outside and down the mountain-like track to where Joe was digging. 'It's coming round,' I said. The smile was one of relief rather than pleasure. 'It is?' and he jabbed his shovel into the ground and came back with me to the hut.

The badger was a patient for six weeks, and every day Joe fed him with bread and milk, then when he got stronger shared his sandwiches. Bish was quite unconcerned and showed no jealousy, and the badger in his turn seemed to accept Bish; and then came the time when the badger, gaining confidence, remembering freedom, began to show restlessness. 'To my way of thinking,' said Joe, 'it won't be long before he's ready to go.' In this he was correct but he did not foresee the manner of his going.

At week-ends, while Joe remained at home, Jeannie and

I used to take over as nurses, and one Sunday evening we fed him as usual, saw that he was comfortable, and shut up the hut. I was first back there in the morning and when I had opened the door, a glance was enough to show the badger had gone. The floorboards had been ripped from the centre of the hut as if a man had been at work with a pickaxe, and as there was only soil underneath, it was then easy for the badger to rejoin the wild where he belonged.

*　　*　　*

Joe used to refer to each meadow as a garden. 'That garden by the quarry is frosty,' he would say. Or: 'I've dug three hundredweight from this garden before May month . . . handsome samples.'

I was in this particular garden one November afternoon during this first year we rented Pentewan, grimly pursuing my task of rotovating the ground. Machines, when seen in a catalogue, appear to perform their duties magically on their own; and if there is a picture of the operator, a broad grin on his face suggests his presence is only a formality. Perhaps it is when the ground is level, but at both Minack and Pentewan the meadows are steep and contracted; and an hour with the rotovator leaves the body pommelled and aching as if it had been stretched on the rack.

The rotovator works the ground downhill and in order to keep the tines deep in the soil, it is necessary to weight the body on the handlebars, at the same time being prepared to lift it if you get warning of an under-the-soil rock. When you return to the top of the meadow you disengage the rotovator, then put the engine in reverse; but in order to control the machine, to prevent the handlebars shooting skywards, you have to do this job by pressing one foot on the cover of the rotovator while hopping backwards on the other; and at all times your arms are also having to force the handlebars downwards. The job is a punishment, a self-inflicted torture which awaits its compensation only when all the land is rotovated, and you rustle the sweet knowledge in your mind that you have achieved in a week what a labourer with a shovel would have done in eight. The pain was repeated twice a year, first in the autumn and then when the potatoes were being planted, the second occasion, of course, enabling the shoveller to dig through the soil at great speed; but it is a November afternoon that I am remembering in a garden that Joe once prized as one of his best. As I performed my routine, the engine roaring, my limbs craving for rest, I saw John in the distance with a pair of horses ploughing the field that edged Pentewan and his own.

At the time, he and I were not on speaking terms, and although he had to come Minack way almost every day to collect his horses or pass on down to his cliffs, he never spoke; and when sometimes in a flush of trying to be friends again I wished him good day, my wish was left to hang alone in the air. On this occasion I observed that when he and his horses reached the end of the field and were ready to turn, he would wait a moment or two, and stare across in my direction. His action irritated me, little realising how fortunate, in a few minutes, it would prove to be.

But I was irritated because I had an uncomfortable feeling that he was not wishing me well; he resented our presence at Minack because he did not consider that we belonged there, and he smouldered with vexation that the roughness of the life had not driven us away. Now we had the Pentewan meadows we had become entrenched. He himself would like to have had them. What right had we to move in and collect such a prize?

Physical effort that demands great strain, I have found, creates a pattern of twisted thoughts, the mind is a daytime nightmare, and while the body is being pounded with exhaustion the brain races with a kaleidoscopic jungle of ideas. Such was the course of my thinking as I grimly continued my labour and when, suddenly, while I was reversing, a wheel hit a rock and the machine lurched sideways.

At the same time the catch which disengaged the rotovator slipped out of position and the tines began circulating with great speed. The handlebars shot up skywards and in this instant of my loss of control, my left foot which had been weighting the rotovator cover was twisted under the cover and met the full force of the tines. The next thing I knew was that the machine had turned on its side, the engine had spluttered to a stop, and the tines ceased circulating because my foot and part of my leg was wrapped round the shaft under the cover.

Tommy, I knew, was in a meadow within shouting distance alongside the Pink Hut. I yelled and there was no answer. 'Tommy!' I shouted again. 'Tommy! Tommy! Tommy!' Heaven knows what he was doing, perhaps drowning my cries with some of his own. I lay there immovable, the weight of the tractor on my leg while my foot, I began to realise, was oozing wet in my rubber Wellington boot.

The shock of the accident was now replaced by panic. There was every reason to suppose that no one would hear me; Joe, I knew, was in one of his gardens close to the sea while Tommy, if in one of his moods, might well have his mind and ears in another world. I was beginning to have pain. 'Tommy! Tommy! *Tommy!*' I was reaching that hazy, never-never land which heralds a faint when suddenly I heard the beat of running footsteps to the left of me. I twisted my head around and through the grass which brushed my face I saw John.

'All right, mate . . . lie still, I'll get the tractor off you.' He had the strength of a bull and he heaved up the tractor as if it had the weight of a wooden chair . . . but, as the tractor became upright, so it became clear that my foot was hooked on a tine like a joint on a butcher's hook; the point had gone through one side of my foot and out of the other.

'If you could find Tommy,' I said, 'he could go over and fetch Mrs Tangye and get bandages.' John gave me a cigarette, then disappeared; and a few minutes later returned with a scared Tommy who went off across the fields to Minack. I soon found that I could not begin to free my foot until the boot was cut away, and this John proceeded to do, sawing away with a blunt pen-knife at the rubber. It was several minutes before he was successful and by that time my principal anxiety was that Jeannie might arrive while I was still trapped. Unfortunately when the machine turned over and the engine stopped, the rotovator was stalled in gear;

and because of the position of the tine that held my foot, my foot could not possibly be freed until the rotovator shaft had been turned several inches. It would not budge.

'You'll have to rock the machine, John,' I said, 'there's nothing else for it.'

At any moment Jeannie would be appearing over the hedge, and I could not bear the thought of her seeing me.

'Rock it to and fro,' I said, 'I often do it when it stalls after getting a stone jammed in the tines.'

He rocked it gently, my leg moving in rhythm, and suddenly the shaft was free. John's cap was pushed on the back of his head, his face was red, the Woodbine dangled out of the corner of his mouth.

'Now be careful, mate,' he said, 'take yer time with the foot.'

It was an occasion when you do not pause to think, for thinking would bring inaction. I noted the shape of the hook, the way it was pointing, the direction I would have to thrust my leg. It was easy. My foot freed itself at the very instant that a startled Jeannie arrived with water, basin, bandages and iodine.

'John here,' I said, looking at Jeannie and aware that he would not want me to show gratitude, 'John got me out of this mess.'

11

I WAS in bed for a fortnight and on crutches or hobbling with a stick for a further six weeks.

Perhaps I should have taken the accident as an omen. What does a shipowner say to himself if a mishap occurs to a new vessel at the moment of launching? I was brought up on the comforting philosophy that single mindedness, a dogged determination to succeed at some specific task inevitably led to conquest; and hence, I remember, I spent hour after hour, week after week, bowling by myself at the nets when I was at Harrow under the misapprehension that it was the road to the Eleven.

That I was laughed at was part of the test, and that I ignored this was part of the philosophy. It is a useful philosophy in the armoury of schoolmasters because boys without talent believe they can gain the same rewards as those who have, and those who have talent are lured to make the most of it. As far as I am concerned the philosophy has lingered in its influence; and the result has been that, although I have often failed to gain the objectives which from the beginning I had no chance of gaining, my efforts have often brought unexpected but pleasurable rewards. Thus, although I am superstitious enough to be wary of Friday the thirteenth and of walking under ladders, and always feel happier if a black cat crosses my path, I consider omens as incidents to forget however moodily I may greet them. Had I shied from Pentewan as a consequence of my accident Jeannie and I would have been spared countless laborious hours and, for that matter, considerable expense; but we would never have tasted the subtleties of the reward for staying.

Obstinacy is, of course, both a virtue, and a fault, and the

151

art lies in identifying the dividing line; and in this tussle of identification you can be called courageous one moment, a fool the next, and brilliant the one after that – if your objective has been achieved.

Our particular obstinacy at Pentewan was to heave our energy and enthusiasm against the weather, and every time it knocked us out, to bob up again, roll up our shirt-sleeves and defy it once more. You cannot treat the weather that way. It always wins. It obliterates a thousand hours of effort in a night, with the same abandoned power of a finger smudging a mosquito on a window-pane.

Should we have packed up after the first wail of defeat? We met a little barrel of an old man in a pub shortly after we had taken over the meadows who for many years had worked the selfsame meadows himself. 'Expect,' he said, in a piping voice, 'a bumper harvest once in every four years.' He did not intend to be gloomy. He was giving the glad news that we would make so much money in one year that it would not matter what happened in the other three. Old men of the countryside appear to novices as oracles; as if the lines on their faces, the horizon look in their eyes, the slow motion of their movements harken a confidence within you that echoes your belief in the Prophets. Thus each time the weather struck we revived ourselves with the words of high promise: 'Expect a bumper harvest in every four years . . .'

We needed, however, that good harvest the first year; and our optimism excited us to expect it. It was indeed vital that it should be a good one. The hazy honeymoon with escapism was being replaced by the conventional necessities of day to day existence, our commitments were increasing, our reserves dwindling. We took on Pentewan knowing it would vastly increase our expenses, but saying to ourselves that if we planned with vision, courage and care, all we would then require would be to have luck on our side; for endeavour, however painstakingly pursued, can rarely receive its accolade unless a magic bestows it.

Yet we were aware that there was something else at stake besides material victory; there was the continuing challenge to prove that we were not flirting with the tedium of manual labour, that our enthusiasm had not been checked by reverses or by the roughness of the life, that we possessed staying power which could earn respect. It was a simple ambition and some would call it a valueless one, but within it there was the prospect of peace of mind born of permanence. There is no permanence in the conventional ambitions that hasten you up the pyramid of power, each step killing one ambition and creating another, leading you by a noose to a pinnacle where, too late, you look back on the trampled path and find the yearning within you is the same as when you were young.

We knew, therefore, that we could not impose ourselves on the countryside but had to be absorbed by it, creating by our efforts an intangible strength that became an element of the beauty, of the wildness, and of the peace around us; and we would then begin to feel and to see the gossamer secrets that are for ever hidden from the casual passer-by. I was about twelve when my father took me to see an old man who lived in a cottage in the woods near Bodmin; why we went or who he was I do not remember; but I remember the untamed setting and how, when we went inside, what seemed to be a cluster of birds flew out of the window. I was disappointed because I had never known birds in a house before, and I wanted to see them flying around.

'Will they come back?' I asked. 'Not till you have gone, I'm afraid,' said the old man, 'you see I've been here a long time and I am accepted like that old fir tree out there.' The incident has always been to me a lesson in living.

My foot had recovered when the time came for planting the potatoes . . . eight tons of them. It had been a mammoth task in the first place, when they arrived at the end of October, to put them away ends up; partly in the Pink Hut and partly at Minack, and as I for most of the time was out of action, the tedious job was shared between Jeannie and Tommy. They were an incongruous couple to be together and I awaited expectantly at home her report on their latest conversation.

'Tommy is in one of his silent moods,' she would say,

'hasn't said a word all morning.' Or: 'Tommy's bought a camera and he's spent the afternoon telling me how he's going to take pictures through his telescope.' Or: 'Tommy's in a terrible state. The police called on him yesterday evening. The camera he bought was a stolen one!' Or: 'Tommy wants us to get a portable tent which he can take along with him as he goes on working in the rain!'

Tommy was undismayed by the quantity of potatoes we were planting, and on one occasion as he was silently putting them away he suddenly roared with laughter.

'What's funny?' asked Jeannie. 'Just you think,' he answered, 'what they are going to say when they see all these going off to the station!' He was foreseeing the harvest, and 'they' were John and any of his previous bosses. 'They won't like it,' he added, 'won't like it at all!'

Tommy was sensitive to the cost of the venture as I had warned him that we would have to take at least £500 before we showed any profit, and that the profit would have to be large enough to pay for our keep and his, for another six months in any case. As a result he became very concerned with the rats which penetrated through the floorboards of the Pink Hut and of the mice which entered the Minack potato hut. 'Every potato they damage,' he said earnestly, 'means a half-crown thrown away next summer . . . we must have poison down all the time.'

Sometimes, mild as the climate may generally be, we have bitter cold snaps which catch us unawares and the frost bites inside the potato huts; as a result some of the potatoes are either squashed into uselessness or are 'chilled', which means they will never grow a full crop. One night Jeannie and I had gone to bed when we heard a knock at the door, followed by Tommy's stentorian voice. 'I've come to tell you it's freezing!' He had walked a mile from his caravan to warn us, and to help us carry the paraffin heaters to the potato huts.

It was, however, a comparatively mild winter and we were able to start planting early in January and carry on, except when it was wet, for day after day until all eight tons were in the ground by the first week in March. We had prepared the soil according to advice from the experts; heavily liming the Pentewan soil in the autumn because the analysis showed it had not been given any lime in years; and dressing each meadow as we came to plant it with a compound chemical fertiliser. Our allotted tasks were for Jeannie to cut the potatoes and fill the baskets, Tommy to shovel them in, while I rotovated a piece of ground ahead of Tommy, carried the baskets from the hut to the meadow concerned, and dropped the potatoes in the drill Tommy had opened up.

These tasks may seem straightforward, but they caused arguments. We were so anxious now that we had suddenly become big potato growers to perform the planting according to the best advice available that we confused ourselves with a plethora of advisers. We were soon told, for instance, that we should be using fish manure and not the compound fertiliser of which we had bought two tons.

'You want body in this ground, not chemicals,' said one esteemed farmer of the neighbourhood. This worry, however, had come too late to concern us; and we consoled ourselves with remembering the opposite view of the agricultural adviser who told us that chemicals were the only fertiliser for the early crop as they acted so much more quickly. Next came the pros and cons about cutting the potatoes. Then the question of space intervals in planting, and how much soil should cover the potatoes. As in other more important matters, the experts contradicted each other. Cut each potato in as many pieces as there are shoots, was the advice of one old farmer who had grown potatoes in the district for thirty years. His neighbour, on the other hand, asserted with equal confidence that potatoes should not on any account be cut, unless the planting was in March. Plant them seven inches apart and fifteen inches between the rows said one; plant them twelve inches apart and eighteen inches between the rows said another. Cover them with plenty of soil, cover them so there is only a shallow layer above the shoots. The opposites briskly met each other and left us bewildered referees.

It is easy to understand that the more you cut the

potatoes, the more plants you will have as a result; and thus greed encouraged us to cut them. But the anti-cutters maintained that a cut potato produced a vulnerable plant, a plant that had no reserve to fall back on if it were pulverised by a frost or lambasted by a gale . . . and Pentewan, its meadows lying facing the threatening sweep of the sea, suffered constantly the prospect of obliteration.

'Ah,' said an old pro-cutter appearing to be wise, 'it all depends on weather.'

This wisdom also applied to the advantages and disadvantages of shallow planting. A potato likes to be near the surface of the ground to bask in the warmth of an early spring sun and, in times of dry weather, to drink the benefits of dews and light showers.

'But,' said a saturnine farmer, 'I've known all shallow planted potatoes be rotted because of a freeze-up.'

Thus, it seemed, the gods had to be on your side if you engaged in cutting or shallow planting, and Jeannie and I were not prepared to trust them. We would play for safety. We would cut only the biggest of potatoes, and we would cover them liberally with soil; but there was still the question of space intervals in planting.

We were, in any case, concerned as to whether we had enough cultivated land for our eight tons; and so the variation between the theories of space intervals in planting were important to us. The difference, for instance, between a seven inch space interval and a twelve inch would mean that the latter would require nearly twice as much land, and then there was still the difference of fifteen or eighteen inches between rows to worry about. Such closeness of planting is a joke to the normal potato grower who expects to have two feet between the rows and perhaps eighteen inches between each potato; but on the cliff it is different. The pundits declare that the more closely the potatoes are planted, the more likely they are to protect each other because the green tops sway in a solid phalanx in a gale, instead of each green top being whipped on its own; and that in a period of drought, the shadow of the leaves hides the sun from the moisture which is in the soil.

Jeannie and I listened to the profusion of advice like foreign students at an English lecture; we made notes, held discussions, but in the end felt lost because experience could be the only interpreter. Nobody seemed to know what were the best methods. There was no standard law. Each season had different growing conditions. Every section of the cliff had a special character of its own; and even the meadows had individual personalities.

'It takes a bit of time to get to know them,' said Joe glumly to me one day, 'and half a meadow is sometimes different to the other half.'

Thus, it appeared, old meadows were as temperamental as human beings; and ours at Pentewan, time seemed to prove, were like overworked clerks in need of a holiday. They were exhausted. After a hundred years of hard labour in producing potatoes, they chose to rebel when Jeannie and I arrived as their masters. The soil was sick of potatoes and wanted a rest; but we in our innocence believe they were the mirror of our future prosperity, and when I dropped the last potato of the eight tons behind Tommy's shovel I celebrated. I was now a big grower, probably the largest grower of cliff potatoes west of Penzance, and I mused happily over my succulent objective – the Cornish new potatoes which would surprise the townsmen like the advent of fresh garden peas, bringing us the cash which would ensure security.

Jeannie holds the view that the pleasantest part of the growing season is when the land has just been ploughed, or a crop just planted. Then there is nothing to worry about, the soil looks clean and rich and the mind is full of comfortable calculations of the prosperity to come. It was in this mood that we surveyed our handiwork of the past two months and each day, wresting time from daffodil bunching, we toured the meadows with Monty trotting along with us. Gradually we began to notice the green buttons bursting out of the soil, and we started to use the language of potato growers: 'The meadow below the gate is in rows' or 'The meadow above the Pink Hut looks backward.'

The Minack meadows had been the first to be planted and

thus the first to be peppered with green but the Pentewan meadows, aided by the extra hour of the sun they received as they stared south toward the Wolf Rock, were quick to catch up. Soon, in the ideal mild weather, the plants were growing so fast that the pundits were talking of the earliest potato season on record; and Jeannie and I rejoiced that it seemed we were scheduled for beginner's luck. John was happy enough to smile and volunteer good mornings, and Joe's boss – the farmer who rented us Pentewan – forgot his quiet self and made jokes. There was a pleasant camaraderie on the cliffs, and confidence that all would share unenviously in the prosperity ahead.

One afternoon, it was Thursday March 27th, we heard a chiff-chaff making its monotonous call, the first of the year, the wonder of its African journey transferred to Minack woods; and it gave us the cool pleasure of confidence in ourselves and our surroundings. The cry followed us: 'Chiff Chaff! Chiff Chaff!' – and the sound of its limited note, amid trees pinking with buds, moss brightening with growth on old rocks, primroses a secret ecstasy unless unexpectedly discovered, pools of ragged robin and bluebells . . . the sound of its limited note derided the tyranny of the automaton age and the warped values that advance the putrid aims of the dodgers of truth, the cynical commentators of the passing scene, the purveyors of mass inertia. The dull two notes of the tiny bird trumpeted defiance of the fake and the slick, bringing to the shadows in the woods the expanse of its own achievement; until the sound gently entered the evening, and as night fell, hid among the trees.

It was suddenly cold, and as I came back from shutting up the chickens a sudden breeze hit the branches above my head, a sharp thrust from the east. Indoors Jeannie was stirring soup on the stove while Monty was behaving as if scissors were after his tail and dinosaurs awaiting his pounce.

'What on earth's wrong with Monty tonight?' And I bent down and tried to pick him up. He darted to the door and when I moved to open it, rushed to the sofa, forking his claws in the side, raking the material, and earning a 'Shut up,

Monty!' from Jeannie. There was a sound outside as if a car was driving up to the cottage. 'Listen,' I said, and we paused, tense. 'It's a plane,' said Jeannie, relieved. There it was again, a rushing, moaning sound. 'It isn't,' I answered knowledgeably, 'it's the wind.'

It was the sound of the scouts, the fingers of the wind, stretching ahead probing the hills and woods, the rocks and hedges, the old cottages, the lonely trees acting as sentinels of the land. They probe and jab, searching for flying leaves, decaying branches ready to fall, for flowers youthfully in bloom, for the green swath of the potato tops; and finding, they rush on searching for more, magnificently confident that the majesty of the gale which follows will crush and pound and obliterate. And when they have gone there is an instant of stillness to remind you of a quiet evening, the passing assurance of a safe world, and you wait; you wait and wonder if you were wrong and the wind is innocent; you listen, your mind peeling across the green meadows whose defences are impotent; then suddenly the slap of the face and the braying hounds of hell and the heaving mountain of maniacal power.

12

THE gale roared without pause till the afternoon of March 29th, vicious, friendless and with frost in its scream; here was man as helpless as the foam on the rocks, centuries of rising conceit contemptuously humbled, the joke of the tempest. Action was masochistic. We struggled heads down as if fighting a way through invisible jungle grass, buffeted, pushed back, soundless in our shouting, kneeling to the ground to gape at a meadow in its progress towards obliteration, then hustled home as if our coats were kites, running without effort, feathers in air.

We sat and waited. The vapid wait, droning the hours away with our fears, calculating losses, listening to the ships' waveband as vessels neared Land's End ('I don't fancy going round the corner'), unknown voices sharing our company, leaping to the window when the noise for a second abated, hearing the sea hissing like a coastline of cobras, sleeping with demons in our dreams. Waiting, waiting, waiting. And when it was over, when our ears were still humming with the beating drums of fury and the sea still heaved in mud-grey valleys, we went out into an afternoon that had suddenly become as caressing as a summer's day; as if a lost temper had been replaced by shame and the cost of havoc was being guiltily assessed.

The Minack meadows were a pattern of black stumps; in pocket-size havens the wind had entered like a tornado, and there were gaps where not even stumps were to be seen. At Pentewan the army of green, the plants the size of cabbages had become a foot-high petrified forest drooping in the sunshine like melting black candles. Black also was the grass on the banks, filmed as if with tar, and the stinging nettles which once taunted us to scythe them down; and here and there wild daffodils stared forlornly with petals shredded into tea-stained strips; or with necks broken, their heads drooped against the stems like victims of the gallows. The desolation looked up at the blue sky and the fleck of a lark singing. A magpie flew by coarsely chattering, and for a second I saw a fox silhouetted on a rock above the quarry. A boat chugged by outward bound to the fishing grounds beyond the Isles of Scilly, and we looked down at the men on deck as if we were on a hill and they in a valley. Normality was returning even if the thrash of the whip was still in our ears; ideas began to form, the warm challenge born of disaster quickened our minds, the sense of comradeship which frays in tedious defeat but sharpens in sudden defeat, became exhilarated, and I greeted Joe as if victory was our companion.

He was standing gloomily by the Pink Hut at the head of the path that corkscrewed steeply downwards to the sea, wearing his mildewed green trilby, an unlit pipe in his mouth and incongruously an old telescope slung from his shoulder. Bish was at his feet and she wagged white body and tail as I approached, whimpering a greeting.

'Does a gale like this often happen?' I asked with mock humour. Joe, after all, had been part of this cliff for seventeen years and he would have the answer to the permutation of emergencies.

'I've known nothing like it,' he said glumly, then grinned as if this might be a shield against the consequences, and went on: 'Coming so late with taties up like that they'll never recover . . . I don't think so, not in time at any rate.'

The tone in which he spoke sent a chill through me. Up to then my instincts had been charging me to get to grips with retrieving the disaster by discovering what wise old farmers would do and by energetically putting their proposals into effect. As simple as that. It was a setback not a finality, and means were available, if I could learn about them, which would put things right. But Joe had talked about time, and time had not entered into my calculations.

Now I suddenly saw that time was the vital factor in any recovery. The cliff no longer held the advantage over the inland potato growers stretching up the country to the great potato areas of Lincolnshire. The cliff potatoes would have to pause, summon strength to send out new shoots, push out into a second cluster of leaves . . . and all this before there could be any question of making actual potatoes. Instead of being ahead they would be behind in the race. The inland potatoes would be still underground or just breaking through, and thus they would continue to grow with the speed which comes of normality; and the avalanche of their harvest would crush the markets while the cliff was still being jabbed with shovels. The prospect scared me.

During the following days inland farmers roamed the cliff in the same way people like to visit and stare at the scene of an accident. They were solicitous, but one suspected their sudden appearance was connected with assessing how our misfortune might result in their good fortune. They got on Tommy's nerves. 'Serve 'em right,' he snorted, 'if they have hard frost after Buryan feast.'

Feast Day was the second Sunday in May and it was traditional that frost be expected up to that date but not afterwards; and so Tommy was wishing them ill at a time when their potatoes would be at the same advanced stage as ours had been. But Tommy's personal chip of revenge was no reply to the predicament with which we were faced. We had gambled so heavily on the prospect of a harvest with handsome returns that failure inevitably would drain the last of our capital reserves. We would either have to return to London or Tommy would have to go, and leave us to carry on with the work on our own. It was the kind of situation which lies naggingly at the back of your mind but which you refuse to accept seriously while an element of hope still exists; and both Jeannie and I could not believe that such total defeat was possible. Our armour was our enthusiasm and, just as useful, our ignorance. We were, therefore, both determined to attack the next few weeks as if energy provided the certainty of victory.

But there was little we could do. Convalescence cannot be successful overnight, nor can plants grow with the speed of those in a nature film; and the only action we could take was to dose the meadows with nitro-chalk. Among potato-growers nitro-chalk is considered a menace by some and a blessing by others. Its purpose is that of a pep pill and given convenient conditions such as warm and damp weather, the effect begins to show within a fortnight by veining the leaves with dark green; thus strength enters the leaves which, on reaching maturity, return it to the developing potatoes. This description sounds like the alluring advertisement of a quack medicine, and it possesses in degree the same deception; for the success of nitro-chalk depends on conditions over which you have little control at the time of sowing. Moreover, and this is the chief objection against it, nitro-chalk though increasing the size of the crop does so at the expense of making it later. Thus if a spell of dry weather follows the time of sowing before rain comes to wash it in, the crop will be later than ever.

'I wouldn't use it if I were you,' said one. 'I'd certainly sow nitro,' said another. My final decision was based on the fact the plants looked so battered and terrible that I felt compelled to take some kind of action to help them; and, as it happened, that was the only satisfaction I had. The nitro-chalk on this occasion provided no sudden elixir of potato life; and to prove it there were two meadows side by side one of which had received its quota of nitro-chalk, while the other had been spared it. Six weeks later the tops of both were still the size of mushrooms, and by this time the grim fact had emerged that the harvest would resemble that of peas rather than potatoes. The plants had been unable to recover, not even our caution in leaving the seed uncut had been able to save them.

We had, however, an ace up our sleeves. It is an obvious calculation that the sum total of man hours required to dig potatoes is the same if there is one man at work or four. Thus one man would take four hours to perform a task which would take four men an hour; and so the pursuit of this idea inevitably led us to the tempting prospect that if we were able to engage two men to help us, the harvest would be cleared in half the time it would take Tommy and myself; and that more extra men would further reduce the time in proportion. Thus, according to this theory, we still had a chance to save the situation by disposing of our miserable harvest when the price was still high; and it could mean, we argued cheerfully to ourselves, that we could take just as much money as with a crop twice the size but half the price.

Our neighbours, however, did not agree with these views. They never had spent any money on extra labour and they were not going to do so now. It was an attitude that pleased us. It gave us an understandable source of contentment that we had a chance to show our teachers that we had the intelligence to cope with a crisis. The problem was, however, where to find the men to help us.

It was now that we had a stroke of luck. We remembered the miners from St Just, Jack and Maurice, who had dug us the well, and off we went to see them.

St Just is a solid town which revolves around the Geevor tin mines and spreads a spider's web of grey cottages with the square as its centre, the sea on one side, and the wild hilly moorland on the others. It is unique for a town of its size in that it is five miles from the nearest railway station, Penzance, and this fact, along with the Atlantic fogs which sweep through the streets in winter, seems to exude a sturdy self-sufficiency among its inhabitants. They are tough, reliable, kind, and aim to see a good day's work performed before they add up the money which rewards it.

Jack and Maurice promptly agreed to help but they would only be able to do so between shifts at Geevor. They therefore proposed they should organise a succession of miners, and that by running a shuttle service in the Land Rover we would collect and return them at times to dovetail with each shift. Thus we could if we so wished collect one group at eight in the morning after the night shift, another at three in the afternoon after the early morning shift, and another at six in the evening after the day shift, the latter working on till dusk. We were also able to engage a retired miner called Willie and a postman, Eddie, both of whom were ready to come full time – the latter taking his annual holiday specially to do so. This galaxy of manpower so excited

Jeannie and myself that we marvelled with gratitude that the fates should so generously come to our rescue.

Within a week we had cleared the Minack cliff, sent away five tons and grossed £250. We were up to schedule both on time and price. But the tight little meadows restricted the use of our full labour force, and only Willie, Eddie, Jack and Maurice provided the extra help. It was a scouting force compared to the army to come, and which proceeded to descend on the larger, sloping meadows of Pentewan.

I now had what I thought was an excellent idea. The method of gathering potatoes in a field is for a tractor to drive its length while the pickers-up are each given a station of perhaps twenty yards for which they are responsible. I decided to adjust this method to the meadow. I fixed the plough and the large wheels on my hand-controlled tractor, gave each miner a station, then grimly drove the machine in such a way that the plough tipped each row to one side where hands seized the tops, shook them, and picked up the potatoes.

It was a method suitable for a flat field, but I had chosen meadows that were square, oblong, round, steep in one direction then in another, with rocks as obstacles, requiring strength and ingenuity even to get the tractor with its large wheels to enter them. Obstinately I stuck to my task, stripped to the waist, my hands ripped with blisters, my body aching with fatigue, dazedly going on and on in the belief that I was the instrument of speed.

It was a delusion. The tractor broke down and when, in its place, shovels were used, the primitive once again proved its superiority over the modern. Two shovellers each took a row, and racing each other up the meadow, they tossed the plants to one side, leaving the rest of us to scramble our hands through the soil bruising our fingers against the stones, chaffing each other with mock accusations.

'Hey, Eddie, have you gone home?' meaning that he had been slower to pick up than the rest of us. Or if a shoveller had sliced a few potatoes as he thrust up the meadow. 'We've got the chips, Willie, so now you'd better catch the fish.' The forced jokes which come with monotonous tasks, remarks which are contrived to bolster minds and bodies which are tiring. 'Dick's in love . . . that's why he's leaving them all behind.' 'Them' being potatoes and Dick being a hunk of a miner who had just got engaged. Long silences, then inconsequent comments on sport. 'Good boy Peter May . . . he's a good boy Peter.'

Periodically Jeannie would appear with tea, cakes and sandwiches, heavy loads which she carried over from Minack, balancing them as if they were jewels while she clambered over the hedges; then a break for everyone, and afterwards Jeannie would join the pickers-up, in shorts, with delicate hands and quicker than any of them. A group had to go back to Geevor and another collected. 'Don't you ever need sleep?' I'd say. 'Well we can last till Saturday.' Tough, cheerful, unsparing in their willingness to help, I felt a tiring sadness that the rarity of their unstinting capacity of giving was tainted by the inevitability of failure.

The price had begun to drop. 'What is it today?' one of them would ask. 'Gone down to thirty-five,' I would answer, and there would be silence; and although they would be getting their pay at the end of the day, such was their rugged, honest independence that they did not feel at peace that they should gain and we should lose.

Jeannie and I became unaware of days and nights, we blazed with the fanatic's zeal to remove every potato from Pentewan in time . . . we were up at dawn to weigh and address the bags, then one of us would collect the first group from St Just, then load up the Land Rover two or three times until yesterday's digging had been driven to the place where Carbis, the St Buryan carrier, would load them on his lorry and take them to the station. Waiting for the post and prices, tea and sandwiches, drive a group to St Just and collect another, more tea and sandwiches, another drive to St Just, then in the evening rough cider with the sandwiches and jokes afterwards: 'Maurice is seeing so many double taties that he can't pick up one.' Then back to St Just with the last group, and because we were both very tired we would go together.

We were aware soon after beginning Pentewan that we

were doomed. Minack meadows had survived in some degree because they were new, the soil was fresh to production and had reserves to face the wound from the slash of a knife, but those at Pentewan were like tired old men who saw no virtue in fighting nor possessed the capacity for doing so. The crop almost uniformly was the size of marbles; and when the shovellers had disposed of a meadow and I looked up in my record book to compare the seed potatoes we had planted and the harvest we had gathered, I found it more comforting to keep the information to myself.

Yet speed might still save us. Jeannie and I clung to the belief that time was our ally, that our town-inspired briskly intelligent ideas would outweigh the true facts. We maintained the illusion until one night, after returning the last of our friends to St Just, we called in on the way home at a pub whose outward fame is its name. The First and Last (pub in Britain), but whose inward fame was provided by the Lancashire brothers who kept it for twenty-five years. 'You've heard the news?' said Jesse Fox, one of the brothers, as I raised my glass, 'taties have hit the floor. They're £6 a ton at Bristol.'

Next morning I looked at Tommy when he arrived, the old shabby clothes, the faded Panama hat, and I said to myself. 'Why does he look so distinguished? It would be much easier if he looked sour and bad tempered.' He performed the motions of his job seemingly unaware that his time with us was at an end. I delayed. When it was all over and Eddie and Willie, Maurice, Jack and our passing friends like Tommy May, nightwatchman at Geevor and collector of sea-debris by day, and Dick and all the others . . . when I had said good-bye to all these, I was faced with the vacuum of telling Tommy Williams that his time with us was over.

I had braved myself to do so when, as I was leaving the cottage, a man arrived whom I had casually met a few days before. He was a brisk, efficient young man possessed with the certainty that his current opinions would secure his advancement. He was like hail on a summer's day, and as I watched him, uninvited, undo his knapsack, then heard him say: 'It's quite all right, don't worry about me, I've got my own sandwiches' . . . I felt only too ready to brain him.

But, and this was the irritation of the occasion, there was a security about his behaviour which mocked the unreasonableness of our own. He represented sense and an arid existence, while Jeannie and I had nothing to show him or anyone else except an intangible happiness. Thus, unknowingly, he provided me with an angry brashness, a reaction to his own normality, when at last I saw Tommy and said I could not pay him any more. 'I knew that was coming,' he said, and his eyes were looking far out over Mount's Bay; 'I'll go back to Birmingham where I was for a time during the war. I'll get a good job there in Birmingham Parks.'

He was down the bottom of the cliff when I told him, and I had a long way up to walk with the knowledge that an unpleasant task had been achieved. I did not feel despair but anger, as if the zest which had led us to the kind of life we had chosen had been stung into fury by conformism pirouetting in self-justification. Ah, you fool, I heard voices mocking, you should have stayed with the herd, the herd breathes safely in the expanse of the plains, its thoughts locked in convention, moving through time sheltered in the security of dullness. The herd does not look for trouble as you have done. The herd is content, it is not greedy like you.

I climbed slowly up the cliff path and found Jeannie waiting for me at the top. 'He took it very well,' I said, 'he's going to sell his caravan and go north. He says he's certain to get a job with what he calls Birmingham Parks.' I spoke with assurance as if I were certain that Tommy was thankful his mind had been made up for him. 'It's funny,' I added, 'but I've always had an idea he hankered after Birmingham Parks and he's only stayed with us because of a queer notion it meant scoring a revenge over the farmers he detested.'

Jeannie did not reply and we began to walk arm in arm up the fields towards the cottage. The silence hurt both of us. We had been consumed by the mission I had just fulfilled, and now we were left with thoughts that frightened us. We had not only lost our gamble, but were faced with retrieving its cost without anyone to help us. We had not bargained for failure when we left London, and its arrival, the sudden barefacedness of its arrival, brought unbearable depression.

And then, just as we gloomily reached the old stone stable and the slope which led up to the cottage, Jeannie suddenly said in a voice that sounded as if our problems had been solved: 'Look! There's a gull on the roof!'

13

THE gull on the roof is called Hubert. He joined Monty as
a witness of our endeavour and the pleasure that has come
with it. He watched us fight back at Minack working for
a year on our own. He saw us beginning to succeed then
rushed by the elements into retreat, then forward again. He
is old now, his feathers have lost their sheen, and when he
gathers himself to fly away he is like a rheumaticky old man
shuffling to rise from an armchair.

He was old when he arrived, or so we thought. 'They
come to man when they're ailing,' Joe had told us, 'you
won't see him for long.' But the years have passed and he is
still with us, and it is only on days when a gale is raging that
he fails to spread his wings over the cottage and alight on
the roof. Then when I see him again I will say, 'The gale
is over. Hubert's back.'

A. P. Herbert came to stay a few days after his first
appearance, and A.P.H. was the instrument which gave him
his name. We were in the main street of Penzance one morning when first one person then another asked A.P.H. for his
autograph. A little crowd gathered among whom was a
young girl who, we noticed, was pushed forward by a friend.
'Can I have your autograph?' she asked, holding out notebook and pencil. A.P.H. bowed ceremoniously, then asked
kindly, 'And whose autograph are you expecting?' The girl
looked at him doubtfully, 'Sir Hubert . . . or something.'
And for that slight reason Hubert became Hubert.

A.P.H. has always remained Hubert's admirer and on this
occasion he bought a gaily painted toy bucket with the idea
of filling it with limpets for Hubert's benefit. He would
clamber down the cliffs to the rocks, spend an hour or two
unclamping the limpets, then return to the cottage where

he would spend another hour cleaning them from the shells . . . so that Hubert could gobble them in a few seconds.

One evening we were listening to a broadcast performance of Cesar Franck's Symphony in D Minor conducted by Sir Malcolm Sargent when Hubert began to cry like a baby screaming for attention. A.P.H. went to the door and looked up to the roof. 'Shush, Hubert,' he said, 'or I'll tell Sir Malcolm.' Hubert miraculously remained silent for the remainder of the performance, and the following morning A.P.H. wrote to Malcolm Sargent to inform him of the incident. A few days later there came a solemn reply. 'I'm delighted to hear of my new and unusual fan. Tell him I hope he enjoys Tchaikovsky's Fifth next Monday.'

Hubert provided us not only with the jest of his companionship but also, in this period of defeat, he showed us the prize of our way of life. This attention from the untamed was an antidote to loss of confidence. It revealed that eyes in the sky watched our comings and goings and now accepted our presence as shadows on the landscape. We were no longer strangers. We had nudged our way into a kingdom that had the passage of time as its passport; no easy short cuts, no synthetic substitutes, no man-made device can breed the trust of the wild. You have to wait.

Others followed Hubert. He remained king of the roof and he would savagely attack any usurper, but during the hours he was absent strangers began to call until they too became friends. They came singly, wary of rivals, plummeting down on the ridge of the roof, then peering into the garden to see if we had noticed their approach. They flew out of the anonymity of the sky, from the vast gatherings on the rocks along the coast, and became in their own way rebels against conformism. We know them now as one knows animals on a farm; and if we are a field or two away and a gull is winging towards the cottage we can often name it by the manner of its flight; or if we are on the other side of the valley and we see a silhouette below the chimney the size of a fist we are quite likely to be right when one of us says: 'Knocker's waiting for us.'

Knocker, Peter, Philip, Squeaker, Gregory, these join

Hubert as our regular visitors and, although sometimes they are away for a month or two, they return and are easily recognised. Knocker announces his arrival by rapping on the roof with his beak, so loudly and briskly that time and again we are deceived into thinking someone is at the door. He has an uncanny sense of knowing when we are in, or perhaps it is that after alighting on the roof he waits to hear our voices before he begins to knock; for we have watched him arrive from afar off and he perches, head erect, waiting; but when we return and go indoors, a minute later the knocking begins.

Peter is shy, he stretches his neck this way and that eyeing us nervously, as if he felt guilty of trespassing. Philip has a confident, lazy, 'no harm can come to me' kind of attitude, and when he is in the mood he will follow us on our walks. Squeaker is a silly bird who has never grown up. He still makes the same piping, wheedling noise that he made when he first began visiting us as a first year bird in mottled grey plumage. He sits on the roof endlessly squeaking, bending his head up and down in the same manner as a nestling demands food from its parents. We throw up a piece of bread, hope for silence, and then when the whine continues I am driven to shout: 'Shut up! Shut up!' And afterwards, when he has flown away, I am sorry I have been so abrupt.

Gregory has one leg, the other presumably lost long ago in a trap; and because the source of his strength is unbalanced he has become barrel chested like a plump duck. He is the easiest to recognise when in flight because his chest seems to protrude like the front cone of an aircraft. He is a lonely gull. I have often seen him attacked by others and driven twisting and turning across the moorland to the sea; and there was one occasion when he was caught unawares on the roof and bullied screaming off it so that he fell in the garden. Hubert was the villain and I rushed out and stood by, until Gregory had recovered sufficiently to hop away to the path and take flight. Usually he calls about an hour before dusk but if someone else is still on the roof I see him waiting and watching in a field across the valley, a white speck against the soil. Then, when the roof is bare, he is with us.

I am wondering now whether I should not have written about Gregory in the past tense. We have not seen him for months. He has been absent before now for several weeks on end, usually in the summer, and we have mocked him on his return. 'You've been cadging from the visitors,' we have accused him, 'you've been hopping on the beach luring them to say "we must feed that poor bird with one leg".' But he has never been away for so long and we are worried. Has a fox caught him as he hopped in a field? Or has his own kind swooped and battered him into the sea?

I wonder, too, whether Hubert is nearing the end of his reign as king of the roof; age becomes driftwood wherever it may be. Once he had only to bellow a screeching warning for any gull on the roof to flee at his approach. But the other day I watched him being himself attacked, pounced upon by a newcomer as he was warming himself on the chimney; and the newcomer, a brash, bossy gull who, without being friendly, greedily demands his food, unbalanced poor Hubert in such a manner that he fell like an untidy parachute to the grass below.

Hubert is fussy. He dislikes shop bread, tosses it in disgust in the air if he is given it, and insists on Jeannie's home-made variety. He loves cheese, but his favourite dish is bacon rinds. 'Let me know when Hubert arrives,' Jeannie will say, 'I've got bacon rinds for him today.' In wintry weather his visits are brief, long enough to have a meal, then he flies majestically away towards the sea, sloping his flight down the valley to the rocks below the cliffs which are his home. In normal weather he may stay with us for most of the day announcing his arrival with a squeak; then he will squat on the wide rugged stones of the chimney as if on a nest, or he will stand looking bored and disconsolate on the ridge of the roof, or walk to and fro along it like a sentry on a parapet. He observes us. We are always aware of his scrutiny.

In the beginning Monty was irritated rather than jealous of him. Monty would doze in the garden, look up when

Hubert started to cry, then curl his upper lip in a soundless snarl. Or if we were having breakfast on the white seat below the cottage and Hubert was strutting within throwing distance of a piece of toast, Monty would lie and stare; then, as if he thought some gesture of defiance was required on his part, he would gently growl like a dog. In time they became friendly enough to ignore each other.

Monty was indifferent to birds and we were never made anxious by the sight of him stalking. He once caught a wren but it was hardly his fault. He was lying somnolent on the grass by the apple tree while a covey of baby wrens flew around him, teasing him as if they were flies and he a tired old horse. I saw him flick his tail in impatience, then pounce, and a wren was in his mouth; but his actions were so gentle that when I rushed to the rescue, shouting at him, he let it go and it flew away unharmed.

He had other temptations but there was a placid quality in his nature that helped him to ignore them. We had, for instance, the usual company of tom-tits, blue-tits, dunnocks, buntings and sparrows flitting about the garden in expectation of crumbs, and he took no notice of any of them; but in particular we had Charlie the chaffinch and Tim the robin.

Charlie attached himself to us soon after the arrival of Hubert, and like Tim he is still with us. He is a bird with a dual character; that of the spring and summer when he is resplendent in plumage of slate-blue, pink, chestnut, black and white wings and tail, is boastful and demanding; that of the winter when his feathers have the drabness of faded curtains, is apologetic, as if surprised he was worthy of any attention. In spring and summer his call is as loud as a trumpet, in winter it is that of a squeak. He has an endearing personality. We may be anywhere in the environment of Minack and suddenly find him hopping about beside us or flitting in the trees as we walk through the wood. We seldom see him any distance from the cottage though once I found him on the edge of the Pentewan meadows. I said: 'Hello Charlie, what are you doing here?' in the tone of voice that might have greeted a friend I thought was in

London. Then, when I started back to the cottage, he came with me.

There was one winter, however, when he disappeared for four or five months and we sadly concluded he was dead. But one March morning when Jeannie was in the chicken run which we had moved to a clearing in the wood, she suddenly heard 'cheep, cheep' from a branch above her head. It was Charlie; and she rushed back to the cottage to tell me. 'Charlie's back!' she said excitedly, 'I must get him a biscuit!' And by that time Charlie had followed her and was sittting on the bird-table cheeping away like a dog barking a welcome. Where had he been? In the autumn hordes of migrating chaffinches sweep along the coast past Minack on the way to Southern Ireland, so perhaps Charlie went along with a group. It does not seem the trip was a success. He has never gone away for the winter again.

Charlie is a diffident character compared with Tim. Charlie never comes inside the cottage whereas Tim will perch on the back of a chair and sing us a song. Charlie, when we are bunching flowers, will cheep on the doorstep of the flower house while Tim is inside hopping about on the shelves. Charlie shies away if you put out a hand, Tim will stand on my outstretched palm until my arm aches.

One November, Tim, like Charlie, disappeared. Tim's territory consisted of the cottage, about forty yards of the lane beyond Monty's Leap, and a field bordering it. One morning a few days after we had noticed Tim's disappearance we observed another robin, a nervous robin, flying about the same territory. Robins, of course, compete with each other for desirable territories, so we looked at this robin and wondered whether he had driven Tim away or moved into the territory because Tim was dead. We did not look with favour; for whatever had happened was distressing.

It was a fortnight later that we saw Tim again. We were strolling along a cliff path half a mile from the cottage when suddenly, perched on a twig of quickthorn, I saw Tim. There was no mistaking him. He was perched with his feathers fluffed out, motionless, watching us. 'Tim!' Jeannie said with delight, 'what are you doing here?' I had a few crumbs in my pocket which I held out on the palm of my hand. A second later I felt the touch of his legs, as if two matchsticks were standing upright.

The following day we returned to the same place. There was no Tim. We pushed our way through the brush calling his name, walking in ever widening circles. At Minack he always used to answer his name. We would stroll a few steps down the lane calling, 'Tim!' – and a few moments later he would be with us. But this time there was no sign of him, nor the next day, nor the day after. 'Well,' I said to Jeannie, 'I hope that hawk which has been around hasn't had him.' Jeannie did not like the casual way I spoke. Tim was as much a friend as any human could be.

You can, of course, always win the attention of birds by throwing them crumbs, and you reap the pleasant reward of watching them; but it is when an individual bird enters the realm of companionship that the soul is surprised by a gossamer emotion of affection. Tim was not greedy. He did not call on us just because he was hungry. I have seen him time and time again flutter at the window of the flower house, then, when we have let him in, mooch around for a couple of hours among the jars full of flowers, warble a little, perch on a bloom with feathers fluffed out watching us at work.

'Where's Tim?' I would ask Jeannie.

'He was up on the top shelf among the King Alfreds a moment ago.'

We missed him when February came and daffodils began filling the flower house again. We would be silently bunching when one of us would break the silence; 'I wonder what *did* happen to Tim?' We knew we would never see him again.

But we were wrong. One afternoon in the last week of February we had gone into the cottage for tea and left the door of the flower house open. Twenty minutes later we returned and quietly continued to bunch. You get in a daze doing the job, picking the daffodils out of the jars, building them three at a time into a bunch, stacking the bunches into galvanised pails where they will stay overnight before they

179

are packed. Your hands move automatically. You only pause to count the number you have done. I had turned to pick out three blooms for the first layer of a bunch when I happened to look up at the beam which crossed the house.

'Jeannie!' I said, 'look on the beam!'

Gazing down at us, serenely confident, head on one side and in best spring plumage, was Tim.

14

HUBERT up there on the roof looks down on greenhouses now at Minack. First a small one thirty feet long and twelve feet wide; then another, one hundred feet long and twenty-two feet wide; then two mobiles, dutch light type glasshouses which are pushed on rails covering two sites and two separate crops in a year, each seventy feet long and eighteen feet wide; and two more the same length but twenty feet wide.

We now work some of the land which John used to have, for John has left the district to go to a farm of his own. Walter and Jack have taken his place; and these two, and Bill who has the other farm which pivots from the collection of buildings, are neighbours who are always ready to help.

We have changed our pattern of growing. Our hands no longer grovel after potatoes in the soil, and we have returned Pentewan to its owner. We have learnt to hate potatoes. Once they promised to be the crop of our prosperity, and instead they have absorbed money, patience and countless aching hours of our labour. 'Once in four years you can expect a bumper harvest,' said the old man with the piping voice when we took over Pentewan. We waited and it never came.

The weather was too dry or too cold or too windy. The weather was always exceptional. 'Never known an April so dry' – and the potatoes instead of swelling would remain the size of golf balls. 'Never known such bad weather in February' – and instead of getting on with our planting we had to wait, knowing the farmers in their fields would catch us up. 'Never known a spring so cold' . . . Every year the old men in the pubs would drag out from their memories their gloomy comparisons. At first it was comforting to know the season was exceptional, then irritating, then a threat to enthusiasm.

As the cost of production has arisen so have the prices fallen. Foreign potatoes flood the markets during the period when those of the Cornish cliff used to reign by themselves. Palates are jaded, and size rather than flavour is the arbiter of purchase. The Cornish cliff new potato is no longer a desirable delicacy; the shovels in the tiny meadows beside the sea, the tedious walks up the cliffs with a chip in each hand, the neatly packed chips being loaded at Penzance station . . . these are the actions of another age. Thus along with the ramarks about exceptional weather, there are those about exceptional prices. 'Down to £30 already? I've never known anything like it.'

We were the first to break with tradition. Others have followed us, and Joe no longer haunts the cliffs that have known him for seventeen years. It is sad when hopes are slowly battered, and events burrow reality into your mind. It is sad, even, when the cause is the humble potato.

Flowers, tomatoes and lettuces are the crops we grow at Minack. We plant every year an acre of winter flowering wallflowers, one hundred thousand anemone corms, a half acre of calendulas and four thousand violet plants. We have fifteen tons of daffodil bulbs. The greenhouses have forget-me-nots, freesias, iris, polyanthus and stocks during the winter; and three thousand tomato plants during the summer. We aim to sell forty thousand lettuces between April and October.

Such is the blueprint of our annual output. Unfortunately, a market garden for the most part is like a factory with workshops open to the sky. The sky is the ceiling. There are production problems as in a factory, selling problems as in any business; but however clever you may be in overcoming these, it is always the weather which dictates your prosperity. Thus I may pay staff for several months of preparatory labour – preparing land, planting, weeding – but lose everything in a hard frost, a few gales, or as in the case of some crops, a period of wet muggy weather.

Or it may be a hot spell at the wrong time which has hit

us. An excessively warm March defeated our Wedgwood iris gamble. The thirty-six thousand which we had planted in one of the greenhouses were scheduled to be marketed before the outside Wedgwood in the Channel Islands came into bloom. But a March resembling mid-summer brought both indoor and outdoor iris into the markets together, deluging the salesmen and bringing despair to the growers. 'Well,' I said to Jeannie, 'we'll never grow iris again.' But we did. The best course a grower can take is to follow one year's bad market with the same crop the next.

Frost, gales, muggy weather, unseasonable heat-waves . . . sometimes Jeannie and I wonder whether we should ever expect normality. Of these frost is the least of our worries, for it is very seldom indeed that there is a persistent hard frost in West Cornwall. Gales, however, will chase us to the end of our days though sometimes they seem to take a rest and leave us in comparative peace. They blow but lack viciousness, or they launch an attack at a time when there are no crops to harm. Such a period lulls us into forgetfulness, and we deceive ourselves into thinking that optimism is a substitute for realism; and so we plant a crop in a meadow which is doomed as soon as a frenzied gale blows again.

The first time we grow anemones in any great number was following a winter that was as gentle as a continuous spring, when our flowers had bloomed in steady profusion and we were happy in the confidence born of success. So confident indeed that we proceeded to act as if gales were no longer an enemy.

We decided that the Dairyman's Meadow at Pentewan would be ideal for an anemone crop, and that another meadow over there would be suitable for the cloches we had recently bought. The Dairyman's Meadow, so called because the use of it was once the perk of the man who looked after the cows on the farm, sloped south, dipping downwards from a high bank to the crest of the cliff. The other meadow, known as the thirty lace meadow because of its size, was more exposed but being flat was exactly what we required for the cloches. We were going to use them as a cover for winter-growing lettuces.

By October the anemones were in full bloom, long stems and brilliant colours; and we congratulated ourselves on our good fortune. 'There you are,' I said to Jeannie, 'it just proves we *do* sometimes know more than the old hands.' For the old hands, in the person of Joe, had warned us that nobody had ever succeeded in growing anemones on the cliff.

That year we had advertised a private box service, sending flowers direct to the home; and the anemones proved such a success that time and again they were specially asked for in repeat orders. We were particularly delighted when one lady ordered twenty dozen . . . to decorate a house for a wedding reception; and she carefully instructed us to be certain they arrived the day before, December the first.

We never sent them, nor did we send any more anemones away that season. The gales had returned, blasting away the illusions that we could grow anemones on the cliff. A monster had roared in from the sea during the night of November the twenty-ninth, and when we reached the meadow in the morning it was as if a khaki coloured carpet had been spread across it. Not an anemone, not a green leaf was to be seen. The meadow was a desert.

It was another monster, three months later, that sent the cloches skidding across the thirty lace meadow. Never before or since have I known a gale which blew so hard as on that March morning, so hard that I had to crawl on my hands and knees in order to make any progress against it. Glass seemed to be flying like swallows skimming the cliff, and there was nothing for me to do except watch and curse and wait.

And as I waited, sheltered a little by a hedge, I suddenly saw Jeannie fighting her way towards me. It was her birthday and I was miserable that it should have begun so disastrously. There was no reason why she would have joined me. I had not asked her nor expected her. She was joining me because it was in her nature that trouble should be shared.

'Here,' she said as she reached me, 'I've brought you a

flask of tea . . . I thought you might need it.' I most certainly did. 'And I've put Glucose in it to help you keep
warm.' I poured out a cup, spilling some of it in the wind,
then took a gulp. It was awful. It tasted like quince. 'You've
poisoned me, Jeannie!' I shouted jokingly into the gale,
'what on earth did you put in it?'

When we returned to the cottage we found the lid was
firmly pressed down on the Glucose tin; that of the Epsom
salts lay loose on the table.

Gales, then will always be our enemy but they are an
enemy which attacks without guile; and it is easier to deal
with a man who boasts his hate rather than with one who
hides it. Muggy weather, warm wet sticky sea fog which
covers the fields like a dirty stream, achieves its destruction
by stealth.

It creeps into the greenhouses sponging the tomato plants
with botrytis and mildew, or blearing the freesias with tiny
brown smudges making them useless for sale. Outside, it
browns the tips of the anemone blooms, and sometimes it
does this so slyly that the damage is revealed only after the
flowers have been picked and have remained in their jars
overnight.

But it is at daffodil time that muggy weather can gain its
great victories. A gale can beat at a wall but on the other
side you can rest in its shelter. Muggy weather gives no
chance of such rest. It envelops the daffodils in a damp
cocoon and brushes the petals, either in bud or in bloom,
with the smear of its evil. There is no defence. You have to
put up your hands in surrender.

There was one year when we lost eighty per cent of our
daffodils in this way, and the compost heaps were piled high
with their stems. The previous year had been a bumper one.
We had bought ten tons of bulbs and in two months had
earned their capital outlay. Thus our expectations were high
when the new season began; but instead, basket after basket
brought in from the meadows had blooms which were un-
worthy of being despatched to market.

This dismal experience had a curious feature, a feature
which only affected those daffodils within a half mile or so

of the sea. First there was a brown mark on the petal, the next day it had turned green, and the third day there was a tiny hole in the same place as if it had been burnt by a red-hot pin. The experts were evasive. They could give us no exact explanation. 'Looks like daffodil flu,' was all they murmured.

Nor could they explain the unhappy events that followed. For two years the affected bulbs were sterile, scarcely a bloom was to be found among them; and those of us who lived on the coast, as well as the Scilly Islanders, disconsolately stared at our meadows of green foliage while growers inland were rushing their blooms to market.

Jeannie had her own interpretation of what happened. Shortly before the daffodils were attacked, canisters of atomic waste were dumped off Land's End; and one of the canisters, it was reported, burst during the dumping. Jeannie blames our misfortunes on its contents being blown back on to the coast mingled in spray. I₋ is as good an explanation as any provided by the experts.

Few people pass Minack at any time of the year, and even at the height of the summer when conventional places are awash with humanity, a figure on the landscape cries out for our comment. 'Somebody's on the Carn!' I'll call to Jeannie . . . Or we will shout the absurd alarm of Alan Herbert: 'White men! White men!'

The occasional hikers plod by, some delighting in the untamed nature of their walk, some indignant that a highway through the undergrowth along the coast is not maintained for their benefit; some stimulated by the need for initiative, some at a loss. 'I've never had my legs so scratched in all my years of walking,' said one furious lady . . . then, as if it were my fault, flinging the threat at me, 'I'm going to write to *The Times*!'

Sometimes we have seen strangers who have had a menacing air about them, as if belonging to the mechanism of progress from which we sought to remain free. Men who have come to survey the district, men walking by who were too well dressed to be hikers, two or three who have spent their days hammering holes in the rocks; and there was one threatening week when an aeroplane flew up and down each section of the coast towing a box-like contraption behind it. On such occasions we bristled with suspicion. Others in beautiful, lonely places have watched such activities, waited and wondered, then found themselves faced with the roar of a motorway, or on the site of some other monument to progress.

One day a man called at the cottage and said he was studying rock conditions in our area on behalf of a certain Ministry. He asked for permission to study those on our land.

'Of course you can,' I said, then added suspiciously, remembering the other activities, 'if you're looking for uranium I hope you won't find it.'

The man stared at me. 'But my dear sir,' he said loftily, 'if I found uranium just think how rich you would be!'

Jeannie was with me at the time and it was she who answered him. 'Had we the choice,' she said, 'between a uranium mine and Minack, I can assure you we would choose Minack.' The man retreated to his duties and Jeannie and I set off to weed the anemones.

We know now there is no possibility of any part of this area being exploited. Buildings and caravans are forbidden, there is no place for a motorway to go, it is too inaccessible even to fear the prospect of an atomic power station; and the scientists have announced the region is bare of uranium. Perhaps I am being over-confident. Such remoteness will always tempt someone to plot its destruction.

But today we can go out of the cottage and shout to the heavens and no one will hear; or lie on the rocks with only cormorants, oyster catchers and gulls as companions; or stroll in the wood with Charlie hopping from branch to branch above our heads, or pause to talk to Tim, or say to each other: 'The gannets are passing along the coast early this year' . . . 'I saw the first whitethroat this morning' . . . 'If you look to the left of those quickthorns you will see a fox sunning itself in the bracken' . . . 'The Seven Stone lightship was towed past this morning' . . . 'We'll have lunch on the rocks and watch the seal in the bay' . . .

These belong to the pleasures which have pleased since the beginning of time. They await in remoteness, hiding away from his intrigue, seemingly insignificant moments their secret in solitude, unhurt by man-made glitter and away from his intrigue, seemingly insignificant moments which enrich the soul. They live with us at Minack so that whatever material disappointments we may have, however hard may be the consequences of a failed harvest, they take us forward again. It is a way of life which belongs to the ages instead of ourselves.

Monty was fifteen years old when he began to ail. There was nothing sudden about his illness, and as the weeks went by there were times when we made ourselves believe that we were worrying unnecessarily. Sometimes he was his old jaunty self, following us in our walks round Minack, then sitting purring on my knees in the evening. We made the customary remarks that are made by those who watch the sick. 'I think the medicine has done him a lot of good' . . . 'He really enjoyed his walk this morning.' And then quite suddenly the sickness within him began to hurry.

He died on a May morning, a morning that was soft and warm and full of sweet scents, the sort of morning Jeannie would have said to me: 'Let's take Monty for a walk before breakfast.' As I was dressing he had begun to cry, and I knew instinctively there was nothing more that we could do. I went away to telephone the vet and when I returned I found Jeannie had carried him out into the sun. He was lying, breathing gently, stretched out on the grass; and, strangely, Charlie was on the ground within a yard of him, Tim was perched on a rosebush two feet from his head, and Hubert was up there on the roof. All were silent.

Monty was the only cat I had ever known and my loyalty was to him and not to his breed. One day during his illness I was telling him that I would never have another to replace him. I was in fact thinking of those sympathetic meaning people who hastened to replace an old friend with a substitute. 'The only exception,' I said, and this I wrote down in my diary, 'is if a black cat whose home could never be traced cried outside the door in a storm.'

190

At the beginning of March the following year, Jeannie and I became aware of a black cat running wild on our land. We scarcely took notice of it except to observe, after a time, that it was always on our land and never on that of our neighbours. But it was so wild that it was only a black dash in the distance.

One evening, at the beginning of April, Jeannie was sitting after dinner talking of Monty. A gale was blowing and rain lashed the cottage. Suddenly I said: 'Did you hear a cry?' And without waiting for Jeannie to answer I went and opened the door.

In came the black cat. She is beside me now as I end this story.

NEL BESTSELLERS

Crime

T012 484	FIVE RED HERRINGS	*Dorothy L. Sayers*	40p
T015 556	MURDER MUST ADVERTISE	*Dorothy L. Sayers*	40p
T014 398	STRIDING FOLLY	*Dorothy L. Sayers*	30p

Fiction

T015 386	THE NORTHERN LIGHT	*A. J. Cronin*	50p
T016 544	THE CITADEL	*A. J. Cronin*	75p
T015 130	THE MONEY MAKER	*John J. McNamara Jr.*	50p
T013 820	THE DREAM MERCHANTS	*Harold Robbins*	75p
T018 105	THE CARPETBAGGERS	*Harold Robbins*	95p
T016 560	WHERE LOVE HAS GONE	*Harold Robbins*	75p
T013 707	THE ADVENTURERS	*Harold Robbins*	80p
T006 743	THE INHERITORS	*Harold Robbins*	60p
T009 467	STILETTO	*Harold Robbins*	30p
T015 289	NEVER LEAVE ME	*Harold Robbins*	40p
T016 579	NEVER LOVE A STRANGER	*Harold Robbins*	75p
T011 798	A STONE FOR DANNY FISHER	*Harold Robbins*	60p
T015 874	79 PARK AVENUE	*Harold Robbins*	60p
T011 461	THE BETSY	*Harold Robbins*	75p
T013 340	SUMMER OF THE RED WOLF	*Morris West*	50p

Historical

T013 758	THE LADY FOR RANSOM	*Alfred Duggan*	40p
T015 297	COUNT BOHEMOND	*Alfred Duggan*	50p
T010 279	MASK OF APOLLO	*Mary Renault*	50p
T014 045	TREASURE OF PLEASANT VALLEY	*Frank Yerby*	35p
T015 602	GILLIAN	*Frank Yerby*	50p

Science Fiction

T015 017	EQUATOR	*Brian Aldiss*	30p
T014 347	SPACE RANGER	*Isaac Asimov*	30p
T015 491	PIRATES OF THE ASTEROIDS	*Isaac Asimov*	30p
T016 331	THE CHESSMEN OF MARS	*Edgar Rice Burroughs*	40p
T013 537	WIZARD OF VENUS	*Edgar Rice Burroughs*	30p
T009 696	GLORY ROAD	*Robert Heinlein*	40p
T016 900	STRANGER IN A STRANGE LAND	*Robert Heinlein*	75p
T011 844	DUNE	*Frank Herbert*	75p
T012 298	DUNE MESSIAH	*Frank Herbert*	40p
T015 211	THE GREEN BRAIN	*Frank Herbert*	30p

War

T013 367	DEVIL'S GUARD	*Robert Elford*	50p
T015 505	THE LAST VOYAGE OF GRAF SPEE	*Michael Powell*	50p
T015 661	JACKALS OF THE REICH	*Ronald Seth*	30p
T012 263	FLEET WITHOUT A FRIEND	*John Vader*	30p

Western

T016 994	No. 1 EDGE – THE LONER	*George G. Gilman*	30p
T016 536	No. 5 EDGE – BLOOD ON SILVER	*George G. Gilman*	30p
T017 621	No. 6 EDGE – THE BLUE, THE GREY AND THE RED	*George G. Gilman*	30p
T014 479	No. 7 EDGE – CALIFORNIA KILLING	*George G. Gilman*	30p
T015 254	No. 8 EDGE – SEVEN OUT OF HELL	*George G. Gilman*	30p
T015 475	No. 9 EDGE – BLOODY SUMMER	*George G. Gilman*	30p

General

T011 763	SEX MANNERS FOR MEN	*Robert Chartham*	30p
W002 531	SEX MANNERS FOR ADVANCED LOVERS	*Robert Chartham*	25p
W002 835	SEX AND THE OVER FORTIES	*Robert Chartham*	30p
T010 732	THE SENSUOUS COUPLE	*Dr. 'C'*	25p

NEL P.O. BOX 11, FALMOUTH, TR10 9EN, CORNWALL
Please send cheque or postal order. Allow 10p to cover postage and packing on one book plus 4p for each additional book.

Name ....

Address..

....

Title ....
(SEPTEMBER)